THE
CONSUMER'S
GUIDE TO

CAT FOOD

*What's in Cat Food, Why It's There, and
How to Choose the Best
Food for Your Cat*

LIZ PALIKA

HOWELL
BOOK
HOUSE

Macmillan • USA

Howell House Book

A Simon & Schuster/Macmillan Company
1633 Broadway
New York, NY 10019

Copyright ©1996 by Liz Palika

MACMILLAN is a registered trademark of Macmillan, Inc.

Library of Congress Cataloging-in-Publication Data

Palika, Liz, 1954–
    The consumer's guide to cat food: what's in cat food, why it's there, and how to choose the best food for your cat / Liz Palika.
        p. cm.
    Includes bibliographical references and index.
    ISBN: 0-87605-722-9
        1. Cats—Food. 2. Coats—Nutrition. 3. Consumer education.
I. Title.
SF447.6.P35   1996   96-37358
636.8'085—dc21   CIP

Manufactured in the United States of America
10 9 8 7 6 5 4 3 2 1

CONTENTS

DIRECTORY OF CHARTS

INTRODUCTION

The idea for this book, and its companion books, *The Consumer's Guide to Dog Food* and *The Consumer's Guide to Feeding Your Reptile*, grew out of my efforts to find the "perfect" food for my pets. My husband and I have always shared our home with a number of different pets and presently have three dogs, four cats and an uncounted number of reptiles. (Uncounted because I really don't want to know!)

Because some of our pets have had special needs, I wanted to find out what dog and cat food really was, especially as compared to the advertisements. I wanted to know what the differences were between the growth, adult and senior foods. I needed to learn how to read pet food labels and to decipher the terminology on the labels.

As I started to understand a little bit more, that small bit of knowledge caused me to ask more and more questions. Why did the dog and cat foods offer such a variety of ingredients? Were some better than others? What was "by-product meal"? Or even stranger, what was "digest"? And most importantly, can dogs (or cats) effectively metabolize and use all of these different ingredients? If they did, why did some foods cause such large piles of feces in the backyard or litter box when other foods seemed to have so much less waste?

I also talked to many other concerned pet owners, some with dogs or cats with particular problems, others with healthy pets who were concerned about what their pets ate. I found that many people relied on what other people said about foods. "Oh, so-and-so has been feeding her dog (or cat) this brand for years." Other people read the labels on foods and tried to make an educated decision. I also found a tremendous amount of misinformation!

As I researched foods, I came to a few conclusions. First, I found that what my pets eat does make a difference. My cats' and dogs' health, activity levels and even mental health seemed to be closely related to their food. Cats or dogs with allergies are even more affected. My Australian Shepherd, Care Bear, would start scratching uncontrollably if he ate a dog food or dog treat with wheat as one of the first five ingredients.

I also decided that there is no one perfect food for every pet. Each cat or dog has its own individual nutritional needs and to make matters worse, those needs can change over the years. The informed pet owner must learn to make an educated decision as to what will work best for that particular cat or dog. Throughout my research, I also found, to my dismay, that many experts disagree (sometimes vehemently!) about dog or cat food. One researcher might state one fact, with research to back it up, while another expert will argue exactly the opposite with research supporting his findings. In most of the situations where experts disagree, I have tried to provide you with both sides of the argument so that you, as a wise consumer, can make up your own mind.

This book was written to give you the knowledge and tools to feed your cat as best you can. I cannot tell you what food to feed your cat. However, I can give you the tools so that you can make your own decision. I have provided you with information about nutrition, cat food ingredients (the good, the bad and the awful), how to read cat food labels, how to contact the cat food companies for straight answers and much, much more.

As you are trying to find the right cat food for your cat, if you have questions about your cat's health, please contact your veterinarian. This book was read by several veterinarians prior to publication; however, it was not written as a replacement for good veterinary care. Instead, it was written to serve as a tool for you so that you, as an educated, informed cat owner, can participate more fully in your cat's health, well-being and longevity.

Liz Palika
and my constant companions and very willing cat food
test participants, Tigger, Troubles, Squirt and Havoc.

ONE

CATS AND CAT FOOD

Cats have been part of our lives for thousands of years. In fact, mythology is full of stories of cats, as companions and as creatures with strange and wonderful powers. In Egyptian folklore, cats were believed to be the descendants of the moon goddess Pasht. The sun god, Ra, was called the Great Cat. According to David Comfort, author of *The First Pet History of the World* (Fireside, 1994), the Egyptians cared so much for their cats that when one died, the owner shaved off his eyebrows, rubbed mud in his hair and grieved openly for days.

Cats had great impact in other parts of the world, too. In many parts of the Far East, it was (and sometimes still is) believed that people, especially the devout, can come back to earth reincarnated as cats. In India, the goddess of maternity was a cat, Sasht. In Siam, when the emperor died his cats were buried with him, alive, but were provided escape routes. When the cats emerged from these holes, it showed his followers that the emperor's spirit had ascended to heaven.

However, the cat has not always been worshipped and in fact, much of the cat's history as a domesticated animal has been very difficult. In the Dark Ages, cats were thought to be the companions of devils, demons and witches and were tortured and killed. In 1233, Pope Gregory IX tried cats (and other pets, including birds) in ecclesiastical courts and convicted these animals as witches. The pets were then excommunicated, tortured and publicly executed. Interestingly enough, Queen Elizabeth I burned cats at the stake for being Catholic heretics.

In the mid-1300s, rats infested with fleas spread across Europe, infecting the human population with the plague, ultimately killing half the population. During this crisis, cats were alternately coveted

1

for their ability to kill rats or killed as a potential source of fleas. Unfortunately, it is believed that cats, too, died of the plague. By the early 1400s, because of the plague and ongoing religious beliefs, domestic cats in Europe were rare, almost extinct.

However, cats started to come back into favor in the late 1500s through the 1700s and more and more cats were being kept for their value as mousers and ratters. Their value as pets started to emerge again, too, and the domesticated cat's luck was changing for the better. In fact, instead of being thought of as the companions of witches or demons, cats came to be known as good luck for sailors. Many superstitious sailors would not serve aboard a ship not carrying a cat. Even today, a cat aboard a ship is thought to bless the ship with good fortune.

FROM HUNTER TO COMPANION

For thousands of years, cats hunted for themselves. Experts at catching mice, rats, birds and insects, cats supported themselves with their hunting skills. That was always a perilous existence, however, and many times the cat went hungry, or the hunter became the hunted, prey to larger predators. As the gradual domestication of cats progressed, those cats who became companions to people were able to share favors. The cat would hunt the vermin that got into stored foodstuffs and in turn, people would share leftover food and would provide protection from larger predators and other dangers.

As we have seen, this partnership had its ups and downs, depending upon the times and the society involved. At times the cat was worshipped, protected from dangers and fed from its owner's plate. At other times, not only did the cat have to forage for itself, but mankind, the cat's former protector, became the cat's worst danger.

Today, mankind can still be a cat's greatest danger but overall, life is looking up. More and more people each year treasure their cats as pets and companions. In fact, today, for the first time in recorded history, cats are more popular as pets than dogs.

Veterinary care has also improved and cats are living longer, healthier lives. Vaccinations are available to protect cats from many of the diseases that used to kill untold thousands of cats. And our knowledge of nutrition is improving, too, allowing cat owners to feed their cats better.

COMMERCIAL PET FOODS

The first known commercial pet foods were prepared in England from the carcasses of horses that died in harness on London streets. Butchers would sell the leftovers—entrails, brains and other scraps— packaged especially for pet food.

In 1926 in the United States, the Purina Company established the Pet Care Center for testing new animal foods. The first Purina dog food, Dog Chow Checkers, was introduced and received rave reviews from Admiral Richard Byrd, who used it to feed his sled dogs in Antarctica. Since Purina already had a reputation for producing good food for domestic animals, especially swine, dog owners were willing to give the new food a try.

Although manufacturers in both England and the United States continued to produce and sell prepared pet foods in the late 1800s and early 1900s, it wasn't until after World War II that the idea really caught on. Prepared pet foods were a convenience, just like drive-through restaurants and frozen dinners, and those conveniences were much sought after by American women after the war.

Most of the early pet foods were meat-based foods, usually beef or horsemeat. Meat scraps were readily available, were inexpensive and it was widely believed by pet owners that cats and dogs needed to eat meat. Although many grains and other nonmeat sources of nutrition were available to pet food manufacturers, often at a cheaper cost than meat, these ingredients were not often used since it was known by researchers of the time that cats did not have the necessary digestive enzymes to break down the crude fiber or cellulose present in grains, beans, seeds or many vegetables.

However, in 1956, a research team working for the Purina Company developed a controllable cooking process called extrusion. Extrusion cooking allowed feed grains to be used in dog and cat foods for the first time. Dr. Thomas Willard, a nutritional consultant, wrote in a July 1992 *AKC Gazette* article, "What Are We Really Feeding Our Dogs?" "Extrusion cooking adds a crunchy texture to the food for better palatability, and is the single most important development in the pet food industry since man first tossed a wild canine a bone over 20,000 years ago."

Purina began nutritional research for cats in the mid-1950s and introduced Purina Cat Chow in 1962. It quickly became the leading dry cat food.

Purina's nutrition experts have six primary areas of study.

1. Palatability is important; the food is useless unless the animal eats it.
2. Digestibility of the food being consumed is also studied. The higher the digestibility of the food, the better the nutrition.
3. Reproduction studies show whether or not the food supplies the nutritional needs of animals being used for breeding.
4. Growth studies determine whether a food will meet the needs of a growing kitten.
5. Maintenance studies determine if a food will satisfy the needs of an adult cat.
6. Geriatric studies follow the nutritional needs of older cats.

Purina also has other studies checking on certain individual ingredients, nutrients or nutrient combinations. Studies may also follow the specific needs of active cats, less active cats or cats with special needs. Since its inception, over 35,000 dogs and 10,000 cats have been raised at the center, allowing the experts to study pets at every stage of life. Other pet food manufacturers have similar centers, including Iams and Carnation, with similar goals.

By the mid-1970s, prepackaged pet foods had become big business; a $1.75 billion industry. This is more than twice what is spent on baby food! In fact, in many grocery stores, the pet foods cover more aisle space and shelves than do baby foods.

SATISFYING CATS AND THEIR OWNERS

Many health conscious cat owners want to share their philosophical beliefs with their cats and may require that their cat eat a vegetarian diet or a food containing no by-products or preservatives. Other cat owners have different requirements, perhaps wanting their cat to eat an all-beef food or a free-range chicken food. Some of these consumer needs are based in a desire to feed a treasured pet the best food possible. Other desires can be unrealistic; however, many manufacturers have strived to meet as many of these needs as possible, hence the variety of foods available.

Cat food manufacturers appeal to the pet owner in other ways, too. The look and smell of a cat food is primarily for the owner's benefit.

Cat owners want the food to look fresh and smell acceptable. Cat foods that come in tiny fish shapes and bright, meaty colors are made so strictly for the owner.

The other consumer is the cat. A food that is not eagerly eaten will certainly not benefit the cat in any way. Of course, some cats will eat anything that is placed in front of them but many more are discriminating about what they eat, and cat owners are sure to notice when the cat is not eating or is not eating the food with its normal relish.

WHAT COMPANIES WANT

Cat food manufacturers have spent considerable time and money researching cat foods and developing new foods with four goals:

1. to meet the needs of the cat's owner
2. to make a food the cat will readily eat
3. to make a food to meet the cat's nutritional needs
4. to make a profit

RESEARCH AND MORE RESEARCH

The development of a cat food is usually years in the making. Many factors come into play: What is the purpose or goal of this new food? Is it going to target a specific population, such as geriatric cats or kittens? What are the proposed ingredients for this food? Are the ingredients readily available? What would the cost of these ingredients be? Who is the target consumer for this food?

When a combination of ingredients or recipe is proposed for a new food, the ingredients are then analyzed. What is the nutritional value of each ingredient and how do they work together? Will these ingredients meet or surpass the nutritional needs of the cats being fed?

Other factors in the recipe must also be researched. In what order should the ingredients be added? How long should the food be cooked and at what temperatures?

When test batches of the food have been produced, the food is again sent back to the laboratory for more analysis for final testing. Once the food has passed this stage it is then produced in limited quantities for palatability tests.

TESTING WHERE IT COUNTS: ON THE CATS

The Purina and Carnation companies established feeding research centers earlier, but other pet food manufacturers maintain kennels, too, including the Iams Company, another giant in the industry. Some cat food manufacturers ask breeders, veterinarians, kennels or catteries to test new foods. The goal is to make sure the cat will eagerly eat the food being offered.

PALATABILITY. At the Iams Animal Care Center, new foods are tested for palatability by giving the cat two bowls, each containing a different food. Technicians note which food was eaten first, which bowl was emptied first and if any food was leftover, which one. The next day, the test is repeated, except the foods are in different positions so the cat doesn't develop the habit of eating from one bowl first. Because a new food may attract (or depending upon the cat, repel) simply because it is new or different, the tests are repeated for several days or even weeks to make sure the food has staying power.

The food is also tested by many cats. Some cats will eat anything, while others can be very finicky. Therefore, most care centers operated by cat food manufacturers keep cats of all ages plus a variety of mixed breeds and purebreds. If the food does not seem to be accepted by most of the cats, it goes back to the laboratory for more work.

DIGESTIBILITY. When a recipe for the new food has been tested for palatability and found acceptable, the food is then tested for digestibility. The cats' feces are analyzed with the nutritional value of the food compared to the nutritional content of the feces. Other tests analyze the cats' urine, again determining what has been excreted. With these tests, technicians can determine how much nutritional value the cat is actually getting from the food.

LONG-TERM FEEDING TESTS. Once the new food makes it this far, it is then fed to various cats for a period of time and accurate records are kept as to the cats' health and well-being. Depending upon the target of the new food, it may be fed to kittens, nursing queens, active adults or geriatric cats.

Controlling studies are often done, comparing similar cats fed a known diet to cats fed the new diet. Researchers measure body weight, growth, blood profiles, skin and coat condition and general health.

These tests may run for six to nine months, even as long as two years. Foods that will eventually be targeted to specific cats, such as allergic cats, cats with specific health problems or geriatric cats, must have additional tests to back up these claims, and that all takes time.

CAT FOOD REGULATORS

THE AMERICAN ASSOCIATION OF FEED CONTROL OFFICIALS. The American Association of Feed Control Officials (AAFCO) was formed to develop standards for domestic animal foods. The association is made up of feed control officials from all 50 states. Although the organization has no enforcement powers, reputable companies follow the nutritional, testing and labeling guidelines established by AAFCO. Foods that meet or surpass AAFCO's guidelines usually state so somewhere on the food's label. You can contact the AAFCO at Georgia Department of Agriculture, Capital Square, Atlanta, GA 30334.

THE PET FOOD INSTITUTE. The Pet Food Institute was formed in 1958 as the national trade association for pet food manufacturers. The Institute acts as a liaison for the industry before legislative bodies, including the U.S. Department of Agriculture, the Food and Drug Administration, the Federal Trade Commission, the American Association of Feed Control Officials and the United States Congress. By providing accurate information to these and other groups, the Institute strives to promote understanding of the role of pets in our society and the role the pet food industry plays as well.

In 1992, the Institute introduced the Nutritional Assurance Program (NAP). This is a self-enforcement program designed to give an added assurance of quality nutrition in cat (and other pet) foods. The Institute had established guidelines for feeding tests for foods; once these feeding tests have been completed according to the NAP guidelines, the food will have on its label a statement to the effect, "Complete and balanced nutrition according to AAFCO procedures." If you have a question about a particular food, you can write to the Institute at 1200 19th Street NW, Suite 300, Washington DC 20036, or call 800-851-0769.

NATIONAL RESEARCH COUNCIL. The National Research Council (NRC) has established minimum requirements for pet nutrition similar to the Recommended Dietary Allowances (RDA) for people. These guidelines are for an "average" cat, but the NRC qualifies these guidelines by stating that these values cannot be taken as an absolute for any individual or breed since needs vary with age, activity, body condition, climate, stress levels and temperament.

OTHER WATCH 'CAT' AGENCIES. A number of other agencies have their proverbial paw in cat food testing, manufacturing and labeling. The U.S. Department of Agriculture watches cat food processing. The Food and Drug Administration must approve the artificial colors, flavors and preservatives that might be added. The Federal Trade Commission regulates and polices cat food labels. Regulation also happens on a state level with agencies supervising pet food manufacturing, processing and transportation.

THE PRODUCT BEHIND THE PACKAGE

You, as the wise consumer, must keep in mind that the cat food companies are also in business to make a profit, and those profits are readily available. Pet foods are big business, taking up more supermarket shelf space than baby food—and only a fraction of the cat food manufacturers sell their foods in supermarkets. Most manufacturers sell their foods through pet stores, especially the giant chains such as Petco and Pet Supply Warehouse. Other companies sell only to veterinarians.

Advertising is also big business. We have all seen the big name movie or television stars promoting their favorite brand of cat food. Veterinarians tell us about the food their cats' prefer. Cats of all sizes, shapes, colors, breeds and mixtures of breeds fill our television screen while they demonstrate their love of a particular brand of cat food. Other ads show the love cats and people have for each other, striving for that "Ooooh!" reaction and hoping that the name of the food will stick in our minds the next time we go shopping.

No matter where the food is sold or how it is advertised, cat food is a multimillion-dollar business, and each company's goal is to get you, as the cat owner, to buy their food. As the wise consumer, you must be knowledgeable enough to choose the cat food that will best suit your cat's needs.

CHART 1
CAT FOOD MANUFACTURERS' TELEPHONE NUMBERS

Alpo	800-366-6033
Friskies Pet Care Company	800-255-8926
Heinz	800-252-7022
Hill's Pet Nutrition Science Diet	800-445-5777
Iams	800-525-4267
Kal Kan	800-525-5273
Nabisco	800-NABISCO
Natural Life Pet Products	800-367-2391
Nutro	800-833-5330
Pet Products Plus	800-592-6687
Quaker Oats	800-4MY-PETS
Ralston Purina	800-778-7462
Sensible Choice	800-592-6687
Technomene Pet Foods Proper Balance	800-982-9802
Techni-Cal	800-265-3370
Vet's Choice Select Balance	800-494-PETS
Waltham	800-525-5273

TWO

NUTRITION: WHAT'S IN CAT FOOD, AND WHY

Throughout history, food in its various forms has been used as medicine. My grandmother seemed to think that chicken soup could cure just about any illness. Almost all human cultures have a number of foods—not just herbs, but everyday foods—that are recommended for certain circumstances. Over the years, these "old wives' tales" have been replaced by modern medicine. Modern medicine developed certain magic bullets—aspirin, antibiotics and so on—and in the process, forgot many of the ancient wisdoms by which mankind survived for thousands of years.

THE PRICE OF PROCESSED FOODS

These magic bullets have indeed increased longevity and cured many diseases, but at what cost? People and their domestic animals are suffering from malnutrition at drastically increased rates and many researchers feel that our overly processed foods are to blame. We are, literally, cooking the nutrients out of our foods. Other researchers are recognizing more food allergies than were previously known, both in people and in cats, and feel that this is due, too, to our reliance on processed foods. Obesity has also become a major health hazard, again, to people and to cats.

We have forgotten many of the lessons those old wives taught us about foods and herbs and how to use them to create and maintain good health, rather than relying on magic bullets to cure existing problems. However, in more recent years, researchers, nutritionists and alternative medicine practitioners have found that many of those old remedies are based in fact: Many foods do have medicinal properties and these properties should be part of good daily nutrition.

This attitude towards food emphasizes its importance because without food, we would die. With a poor diet, one that does not meet our nutritional needs, we may live, but we will not live as long or as well. With a good diet that does satisfy our nutritional needs, our odds of living better are drastically increased. The same applies to our cats.

GOOD FOOD EQUALS GOOD HEALTH

Before you go shopping for cat food, it is vital that you have an understanding of good nutrition and how it affects your cat's health. Good nutrition is needed for a strong immune system, reproduction, lactation and normal growth. Foods supply the needed substances that act as regulators for the body's many processes, including organ development and functions. Food is necessary for disease resistance, for healing and as a source of energy so that the cat can function and live from day to day.

Nutrition is the relationship between food and the health of the body. The body—in this case, your cat's—takes in food and through chemical changes, digests the food. Cats are carnivores; in other words, cats have sharp, flesh-tearing teeth, a simple stomach and a short digestive tract; all symbolic of carnivores.

Carnivores, by definition, eat meat. Meat or animal protein is more easily digested by cats than protein obtained from other sources. However, even carnivores eat vegetables and other grains. Wild and feral cats, as well as domesticated cats that have access to the outdoors, will often eat the partially digested plant products found in the entrails of their prey. That may seem disgusting to us, but it is natural to the cat. Carnivores are also opportunists, eating anything that is available, including fresh greens, berries and fruits.

THE DIGESTIVE PROCESS

All of the foods eaten by the cat must be broken down by the body into simpler chemical forms. This process is called digestion. With cats, active digestion starts in the stomach where food is mixed with gastric juices containing enzymes that break up protein, fat, carbohydrates and other substances.

As the food passes into the small intestine from the stomach, some of the food, which is now changing into simpler chemical forms, is absorbed into the body. Depending upon the nutrient, some of the food is absorbed into the bloodstream through tiny blood vessels in the small intestine. Other nutrients are channeled through the lymph system. During this part of digestion, water-soluble vitamins are picked up by the bloodstream.

The liver also plays an important part in the digestive process by changing some of the nutrients into products needed by the individual cells. Other nutrients are stored by the liver for future use.

At this point in the digestive process, the cat is now metabolizing some of its food. Lavon J. Dunne said in the *Nutrition Almanac: Third Edition,* "The process of metabolism involves all of the chemical changes that nutrients undergo from the time they are absorbed until they become part of the body or are excreted from the body." Those chemical changes are incredibly complex. The body is constantly working with these nutrients, constructing body chemicals such as blood, enzymes and hormones, or breaking down compounds to supply the cells or body with energy.

The feces excreted by the cat are body wastes, i.e., normal waste material produced by the cat's body plus undigested food material. When digestibility studies are undertaken to analyze the digestibility of a particular food, the feces are analyzed. The formula is, stated very simply, the amount of nutrients ingested minus the amount of food in the feces, which equals the apparent digestibility of the food.

FACTORS AFFECTING GOOD NUTRITION

Proper nutrition, for cats, means that all of the body's essential nutrients are being supplied by the food that is being eaten, in a form that the cat's body can use. Those needs include appropriate amounts of protein, fat, carbohydrates, vitamins, minerals and, of course, water.

Each individual cat, of every breed or mixture of breeds, will have slightly different needs for good nutrition. Things that affect nutrition include:

- the cat's age
- its genetic heritage
- state of general health
- whether or not it is being used in a breeding program

- its activity level
- climate
- stress levels
- the food the cat is normally eating

AGE. Nutritional needs vary dramatically with the cat's age. Active, rapidly growing kittens require significantly higher protein levels than do adult or older cats. Older cats, especially those with weak or diseased kidneys, will require less protein or protein that is more easily digested.

HERITAGE. Just as cats from different parts of the world developed in slightly different ways, with slightly different shaped skulls, or body types, coat lengths or colors, so, too, did many breeds develop different nutritional needs. While some cats will thrive and prosper on a mostly fish diet, others may do better with beef, turkey or chicken.

GENERAL HEALTH. Nutritional needs can vary dramatically depending upon the cat's health. A cat stressed by injury or disease will need more support from a good food to provide for the increased needs of the immune system, and for healing. A cat that is carrying a heavy load of parasites, either internal (roundworms, tapeworms, etc.) or external (fleas or ticks), will need medical attention to fight off the parasites and will need nutritional support to regain good health. Good nutrition can also work towards preventing many health problems by helping to keep the immune system running properly.

REPRODUCTION. Good nutrition is necessary for both the male and female, both prior to breeding and during. The stud cat that is not well nourished may not produce viable sperm and may even have a reduced desire to breed.

If the queen (female used for breeding) is not well nourished, she may not ovulate properly, may not release eggs or may not have the reserves herself to adequately nourish the growing embryos. During gestation and lactation, the queen will be robbing her own body of nutrients to satisfy the growing kittens' needs. It's important that her state of health prior to breeding is good and that her nutritional needs are met before breeding, during gestation and during lactation.

ACTIVITY LEVELS. Most of the older breeds of cats were, at some point during their history, used for rodent control. The Norwegian Forest Cat, the Russian Blue, the American or Domestic Shorthair and the Tonkinese are known to be active hunters. When indoors and with stimulation in their environment—interaction with people in the household—these cats can be quite active, especially when young.

However, many other breeds have been designed as companions, housepets and for the show ring. Some of these breeds are very sedentary, quiet and some have even lost their desire to hunt. Some Persians, for example, have been known to befriend mice; something no American Shorthair would ever acknowledge doing! Other breeds are simply calmer and quieter by nature, like the British Shorthair.

All cats need exercise, though, even cats who live entirely indoors and may have never seen a mouse. Exercise stimulates digestion, strengthens blood vessels and muscles and imparts vigor to all of the body's organs. Although exercise increases the body's need for good nutrition, a cat who plays hard will be more mentally alert and physically healthy.

CLIMATE. The climate in which the cat lives, works or plays will have considerable bearing on its nutritional needs. In cold weather, the cat may need twice the calories needed in warmer weather, both because it needs the calories to keep warm and because it will probably be more active when it is colder.

Even indoor cats will react differently to the changes in seasons and weather. The environment inside our home changes according to the weather outside and that can affect the cat's behavior, activity levels and nutritional needs.

STRESS. Stress can be many things to a cat; it can be the move to a new house, the addition of a family member, increased activity, cat show competition or to some cats, even a new piece of furniture. Some cats are more accepting than other cats, rarely reacting with stress to the environment around them. Other cats are easily stressed. These cats should be fed a diet with slightly higher protein and fat levels, especially during times of stress.

FOOD. The food your cat is eating can cause stress, too, especially if the food is of poor quality, is made up of ingredients that are not easily digestible or if it is simply not the right food for your cat. Food can also cause problems if the cat's diet is abruptly changed, which can cause gastrointestinal disorders and diarrhea. Too much or too little food can be a problem, too, for obvious reasons.

FOOD AND THE BODY

There is no single thing that can ensure good health. Good health is a jigsaw puzzle with many pieces to it. Regular daily exercise, emotional security and adequate rest are pieces of the puzzle. Heredity certainly is a part of the puzzle; a cat that is descended from healthy, sound parents and grandparents will have more of a chance of good health. An environment relatively free of physical dangers, excess chemicals and insecticides will also aid in the maintenance of good health. And, of course, good nutrition is an important part of the puzzle.

Your cat's immune system is a marvel, even to researchers who spend their careers studying it. The immune system is an army that fights viruses, bacteria and disease. Every breath brings with it potentially deadly warriors, ready to strike, as does the dirt in the backyard or the water sitting out in an open dish. Even an old toy, laying in the middle of your living room can be, and probably is, covered with bacteria that could, without a healthy immune system, cause untold trouble.

An immune system can be weakened by inadequate nutrition, and this could lead to a variety of disorders or can make existing disorders more serious. On the other hand, a strong immune system, backed up by a healthy diet, can fight existing diseases and can work alongside the medical treatments prescribed by your cat's veterinarian.

ALLERGIES AND FOOD

Cats are not known to have as many allergies as people or dogs, but allergies are certainly not unknown. Allergies are a case of the immune system overreacting. The immune system recognizes an antigen (a foreign substance) and produces antibodies to fight it. When it recognizes that substance again, later, it overreacts and an allergic response is the result.

Some allergies are inhalants: The allergen is inhaled during breathing. Other allergies are contact allergies, caused, as the name implies, by contact with the allergen, such as grass. Still other allergies might be caused by food or an ingredient in the food. Food allergies might cause an instant response, with swelling of the mouth or throat, or there might be a delayed reaction, such as gas or bloating that appears several hours later. Even more delayed reactions, appearing days after ingesting the wrong food, are common but less recognized because they are harder to pinpoint.

Food allergies may show up as small red bumps that cause the cat to scratch or bite at itself, damaging the skin and leaving it open to secondary infections. With food allergies, the skin may itch all over, but the most common areas of sensitivity are the feet, ears and sometimes the base of the tail.

These are not the only symptoms of allergies, though, they're just the most common. Other symptoms include joint pain and stiffness, epilepsy, weakness, fatigue, bowel disease, kidney inflammation and kidney disease. Cats with food allergies may also suffer from behavioral problems, including hyperactivity, anxiety, fear, depression and restlessness, although the most common is aggressive behavior.

Theron Randolph, MD, a physician and researcher, stated that hidden or delayed onset food allergies are "the most common undiagnosed illness in medicine today." Diagnosis may be made through blood tests and/or feeding trials. In either case, if you suspect a food allergy, contact your veterinarian.

CANCER AND FOOD

Cancer is a word that strikes terror into the hearts of many people. There is much that researchers know about cancer and much, much more that is not known. We know that cancer cells can grow very rapidly, can create their own blood supply and can invade local tissues. Books have been written about the various types of cancers, but using very simplistic definitions, these abnormal growths are called tumors. Those that are relatively harmless are said to be benign; those that spread and damage surrounding tissues are said to be malignant.

Many researchers feel that every living body (human, feline and otherwise) has some cancer cells. Normally, the body's immune system reacts to these cells and either destroys them, inhibits their spread or, in some other yet unknown manner, prevents them from forming tumors. Cancer results when the immune system, for whatever reason, fails to react to the forming cells.

Dr. Gregory Ogilivie, of Colorado State University College of Veterinary Medicine and Biomedical Sciences, studied dogs with lymphoma, and found that cancer changes the way a dog uses or metabolizes nutrients. In a three-year study, dogs treated for lymphoma with conventional chemotherapy were fed a special diet. The diet didn't cure the lymphoma, but it did extend life for anywhere between nine months and a year. Studies have shown similar results for people, and although it is not yet known if cats would have the same reaction, many researchers believe that it is very possible.

Unfortunately, there are no known foods that will cure cancer, and the only prevention is to make sure the cat is eating a nutritious diet that will keep the immune system strong and healthy.

CARDIOMYOPATHY

Heart disease is relatively common in older cats. Rather than having heart attacks, as people do, cats usually suffer from a weakening of the heart muscle. Sometimes the heart rhythm is off, either too fast or too slow. Special diets and medication can often help control heart disease so that even though it cannot be cured, the cat can live a little longer with a good quality of life.

But not all heart disease is caused by age. Dilated cardiomyopathy (DCM) is a disease of the heart muscle, where the heart ventricle dilates, preventing the heart from working properly. DCM is often caused by a taurine deficiency. Taurine is an amino acid that is present in adequate amounts in all good quality, meat-based (or taurine-supplemented) cat foods; however, that doesn't mean that the cat is metabolizing it. Cats with DCM are usually put on a taurine supplement in addition to a special food for cats with heart disease.

DENTAL HEALTH

Jim Humphries, DVM, states in his book, *Dr. Jim's Animal Clinic for Cats* (Howell Book House, 1994), that "over 85 percent of all cats over the age of four years suffer from dental problems." Dental disease is more than just bad breath, it also means gum damage, tooth loss and, if it progresses, even heart and kidney damage. Regular at-home dental care (brushing) can help prevent early dental problems, but veterinary check-ups are needed, too, especially for older cats.

Although what the cat eats will not eliminate dental problems, a good diet can help in a couple of ways. First, good nutrition will help the immune system cope and second, hard kibbles can physically help scrape food particles off the teeth.

FELINE UROLOGICAL SYNDROME (FUS)

Feline Urological Syndrome (FUS) is a troubling disorder that has been said to be nutritional in nature, although some researchers believe the tendency towards it is genetic. In FUS, crystals form in the cat's urine. These crystals irritate the bladder and urethra, causing redness, swelling, itching, burning and bleeding. Symptoms include frequent urination or frequent trips to the litter box with little or no urine passed, blood in the urine, loss of appetite and depression.

The crystals in the urine are made up of magnesium and phosphorus that have been ingested as part of the cat's food. Cats diagnosed with FUS should eat a special food specifically for this problem, such as Hill's Science Diet c/d, which restricts these and other minerals that can lead to crystal formation. These foods also lead to a more acidic urine, which can dissolve the crystals. (Chapter Four has more information about FUS, magnesium, ash and the other minerals involved.)

GASTROINTESTINAL DISORDERS

Gastrointestinal disorders can be caused by a variety of problems, including parasites, infections, metabolic imbalances, tumors, injuries or allergies. Cats that raid the trash can and ingest meat wrappers usually end up with gastrointestinal disorders, sometimes needing surgery to remove the foreign object. Cats (or kittens) that play with strings, threads or ribbons can swallow the toy and cause severe injury to the gastrointestinal tract, usually requiring surgery.

The most common cause of gastrointestinal disorders is usually caused by what the cat eats. The outside cat who eats the mouse, rat or bird that it catches can suffer afterwards. Feeding a poor quality food, a spoiled food or changing the cat's brand of food too quickly can cause an upset stomach or diarrhea. Although some cats seem to have cast-iron stomachs that can handle anything and everything, many cats will become ill when eating spoiled food, especially when raiding the trash can or eating an inferior quality cat food.

Years ago, and even today in some areas, it was common practice to feed cats meat. However, researchers now know that raw meat—even meat sold for human consumption—can contain parasites or pathogenic bacteria that can seriously endanger good health. Although many cats relish raw meat, it should only be given in certain, specific instances, such as to tempt a sick or injured cat into eating.

Even though what the cat eats can often be the cause of gastrointestinal disorders, a good diet can also act to help heal those same disorders. Boiled meat—such as ground chicken or lamb—can be mixed with cooked, whole grain rice to make a soft bland diet that can be very soothing to the digestive tract. This is not a long-term diet, but instead, is for feeding until the cat's intestinal tract is functioning normally again. Then, a good quality cat food should be introduced to the cat over a period of three weeks.

OBESITY

Obesity is one of the most commonly seen problems in cats. Overweight cats are more prone to diabetes, heart disease and many other health disorders. Dr. Jim Humphries, author of *Dr. Jim's Animal Clinic for Cats* (Howell Book House, 1994), says, "Many owners love their pets to death by feeding them far too many treats. Fat cats are prone to some serious medical problems. Obesity puts extra stress on the cat's heart, aggravates arthritis and other joint problems, and increases the risk associated with surgery." He continues by saying that overweight cats also have more problems with the gastrointestinal tract, are more prone to liver disease and even dermatitis.

THE EFFECTS OF THYROID

Hyperthyroidism is the overproduction of hormones by the thyroid gland. Symptoms might include nervousness, fatigue, weight loss and rapid pulse. Hypothyroidism is the underproduction of hormones and results in decreased appetite, dull, dry coat, clumsiness, lack of vigor and, in breeding males, lowered sperm count.

Although both types of thyroid disease can be inherited or can be caused by other factors, nutrition can also be a cause. Many cat foods contain soybeans and soybean meal, both of which are incomplete protein sources, lacking several essential amino acids. If this loss isn't made up for with other ingredients, this amino acid loss could lead to a lack of tyrosine, the amino acid that stimulates the thyroid gland to produce more hormones. Although studies investigating this relationship are continuing, cats with thyroid disease or a genetic predisposition to it should avoid foods high in soy.

EATING RIGHT FOR A LIFETIME

Although many things contribute to how long a cat will live, including heredity, environment and general health, good nutrition has been linked by several studies to longevity. A diet that supplies the cat's nutritional needs is imperative to good health, which in turn, goes hand in hand with long life. Feed your cat well, and increase the chances that you will hear that purr reverberate for many more years!

THREE

THE BASIC BUILDING BLOCKS
OF FOOD

There are eight basic building blocks of nutrition that are present in the food your cat eats. They are:

- water
- enzymes
- protein
- carbohydrates
- fats
- fiber
- vitamins
- minerals

These nutrients contain chemical substances that affect the body. They might provide the body with energy or might assist in the regulation of body processes or they might provide for the growth and repair of tissues.

Each of these nutrient building blocks has its own purpose, its own function, but it does not work alone. All of the nutrients are required, in varying amounts, for a well-balanced diet. The amounts needed are variable, depending upon the cat and factors like age, general health, activity level, temperament and environment (as discussed in Chapter Two).

In this chapter, we will discuss six of the eight basic building blocks:

- water
- enzymes
- protein
- carbohydrates
- fats
- fiber

In Chapter Four, we will continue with vitamins and minerals.

WATER: THE MAGIC LIQUID

A simple substance, water is one of the most abundant and important resources of our planet and one that is taken for granted more than anything else. However, without water, life as we know it would cease to exist.

The adult cat's body is approximately two-thirds water. Blood is slightly over 80 percent water, muscles are over 70 percent water and the brain is almost 75 percent water. Even bones are 20 percent water.

Water is required for the normal functioning of every cell in the body. Respiration, digestion, metabolism and elimination all require water. Water is needed to dissolve and transport nutrients. Water keeps all things in balance; only oxygen is more necessary to preserve life.

A certain amount of water is lost each day through respiration and elimination and must be replaced. The amount of water needed by each cat can vary depending upon the size and age of the cat, its activity level and the climate, especially the temperature.

Dehydration occurs when the cat is losing more water than it is taking in and in severe, untreated cases, can be fatal. If water is available to them, mildly dehydrated cats will usually drink on their own. However, moderate to severely dehydrated cats may refuse to eat and drink and in these cases, need veterinary treatment and intravenous fluids immediately. Because water is so vital, cats should be allowed free access to clean water at all times.

ENZYMES: THE ESSENTIAL BUILDING BLOCKS

Enzymes have numerous essential functions in the cat's body; so many, in fact, that the cat couldn't live without them. Enzymes are made up of two parts; one part is the protein molecule and the other is called the coenzyme. This coenzyme may be a vitamin, or a chemical derivative of a vitamin. Enzymes work by initiating a chemical reaction so that other substances can do their job.

The digesting and metabolizing of food requires a complex system of enzymes to make sure that thousands of different chemical reactions happen as they should. In the digestive processes, an enzyme is capable of breaking down one specific substance. For example, an enzyme designed to break down carbohydrates does not metabolize fats and the enzyme that breaks down milk products does not break down carbohydrates.

In cats, the four basic digestive enzymes are:

- *Proteases,* which break down protein;
- *Amylases,* which break down carbohydrates;
- *Lipases,* which break down fats and
- *Cellulases,* which break down vegetable matter.

By "breaking down" the food, the nutrients in the food then become available for use by the body.

Because enzymes are made up of proteins and other substances, usually a vitamin, the number of enzymes available for use by the cat can vary and can be dependent upon the cat's diet. However, enzyme supplements are available and will be discussed in Chapter Eight.

WILLARD WATER

"Willard Water" is named after its founder, Dr. John Willard, a professor emeritus of chemistry at the South Dakota School of Mines and Technology. Dr. Willard discovered he could change the molecular structure of ordinary water, to which he added fossilized organics. Willard Water has been credited with aiding crop growth, de-stressing cattle, healing abrasions, reducing scarring and conditioning hair. Ask your health food store about ordering Willard Water, or call L&H Vitamins in Long Island City, New York, at 800-221-1152.

PROTEIN: THE FOUNDATION FOOD

Next to water, protein is the most plentiful element in an animal's body, representing approximately 50 percent of each cell in the body. Proteins are incredibly diverse; serving as building blocks of hair, claws, skin, muscle, tendons, cartilage and other connective tissues. Protein is one of the most important elements of food for growth, development and repair of body tissues, sexual development and metabolism. Proteins are also vital parts of the bloodstream, the immune system, the digestive system, hormone production and much, much more.

AMINO ACIDS. During digestion, amino acids are formed when large protein molecules are broken down by chemical action into smaller molecules. Amino acids are interesting molecules; they are both the end product of protein digestion and also the molecules from which protein can be constructed.

Amino acids are vital to the transmission of nerve impulses and as a result are needed for muscular contractions and for the electrical impulses in the brain and spinal cord. Amino acids are involved in the formation of DNA and in the functioning of the immune system. The body's chemistry is so interwoven and so dependent upon other substances and chemicals, that an imbalance of even one amino acid can throw the whole system out of kilter.

Some amino acids are produced by the body, these include *alanine, glycine, serine* and *tyrosine*. Other amino acids are not produced by the body and must be supplied by food. These essential amino acids include *arginine, histidine, leucine, lysine* and *valine*.

Taurine is an amino acid that is essential to your cat's good health. It is involved in the development of many of the body's tissues, especially the electrically active tissues of the nervous system, brain and heart. Your cat can get taurine from animal sources such as chicken, beef and other meats. Commercial cat foods that use plants or grains as the primary protein sources usually add taurine supplements to the food.

COMPLETE AND INCOMPLETE PROTEINS. Protein sources that contain all of the amino acids, such as lean meat, whole eggs or milk, are called complete protein sources. Sources of protein which do not contain a balanced amount of amino acids, such as soybean, wheat or corn, are called incomplete proteins. Besides being a major building block in your cat's body, protein can also be used as a source of heat and energy. When fats or carbohydrates are not available for use by the body in times of need, protein can be metabolized in their place. In addition, excess protein that is not needed for body functioning or repair can be converted into fat by the liver and stored for future use.

GETTING THE AMOUNT RIGHT. Too much protein is not usually a problem in young, active cats except that in extreme cases, too much might cause a fluid imbalance. Usually the cat's body can metabolize the excess protein and store it for future use. However, older cats or cats deficient in a specific amino acid might have problems with too much protein, with potentially serious results, including possible kidney failure. Therefore, excess protein is not advised—more is NOT better in this situation.

Protein deficiencies may result in growth abnormalities, especially skeletal deformities. The skin and coat may also be affected, depending upon the extent of the deficiency, with the coat appearing thin, dull and lifeless. Protein deficiency may also show up as a lack of energy and stamina, mental dullness and even depression. With protein deficiency, there will also be a noted weakness of the immune system and the cat will be open to infection and disease.

SOURCES OF PROTEIN. Cat foods supply protein from a number of different sources; some, as discussed above, are complete proteins, containing all of the essential amino acids, others are not. Along the same lines, some of the protein sources are more digestible (more usable) by the cat than others. For these and other reasons (including cost to the manufacturer and availability) most cat foods have more than one source of protein.

Beef, chicken, turkey or lamb are the most common meat sources of protein. Frequently, cat foods also use fish as a protein source. A few cat food manufacturers use pork. Meat by-products—meat and bone meal, liver, organ meats and other meat products—are protein sources, as well as eggs, milk and milk products, including whey and cheese.

Most cats can actually only digest and metabolize between 60 and 75 percent of the meat they eat. The cats digestive system is not known to be particularly effective. To make matters worse, many of the meat by-products are not as easily metabolized and much of it is wasted. Also, the high temperatures used to process the food reduces the overall protein quality.

Many different vegetable proteins are also commonly used, including wheat in various forms (whole wheat, wheat germ, wheat flour), corn, rice, soy, barley and other grains. Some cat foods will include alfalfa meal, carrots, peas, beans or potatoes.

CARBOHYDRATES: THE ENERGY BUILDING BLOCKS

Carbohydrates are the major element in most plants, accounting for 60 to 75 percent of the dry matter weight of plants. Like proteins, carbohydrates have more than one use in the cat's body.

- Carbohydrates supply energy for bodily functions and are needed to assist in the digestion of other foods, especially fats.
- Carbohydrates help regulate protein and are one of the most important sources of energy for muscular exertion.

Most carbohydrates present in foods are *sugars, starches* and *cellulose.*

Sugars and *starches* are easily digested and are converted to a simple sugar, such as glucose. This is used by the body as fuel for the muscles, as well as the brain and the nervous system. Excess glucose (sugar from plant material) is converted to glycogen and is stored in the liver and muscles for future use.

Cellulose is not easily digested by the cat and serves as fiber for water regulation in the large intestine, aiding in the formation and elimination of feces.

As previously discussed, proteins and carbohydrates can both supply energy to the cat's body. However, proteins have other functions that carbohydrates do not. Therefore, when adequate carbohydrates are present to meet energy needs, proteins can then be used by the body to serve other functions. Too few carbohydrates, and the body will tap into protein reserves to fulfill energy demands.

The cat's carbohydrate needs depend upon many variables, including general health, activity level and energy needs. A carbohydrate deficiency may produce a loss of energy, weight loss, poor condition, depression and a breakdown of essential body protein.

SOURCES OF CARBOHYDRATES. Vegetables and grains that supply proteins to the cat can also be a good source of carbohydrates. Corn, rice, oats, potatoes and wheat are easily digested by the cat after processing and are good sources of carbohydrates.

FAT: THE "GOOD COAT" BUILDING BLOCK

Most cat owners have heard, somewhere, that fats are necessary for a cat to have a shiny, healthy coat. That statement is partly true; a fat deficiency will show up as dry, flaky skin. However, fats in the diet do more than create a shiny coat and all fats are not the same.

Dietary fats, called *lipids,* are a group of compounds that are not soluble in water and have a number of different functions in the cat's body. Some lipids are a part of cell structures, others are a part of the blood plasma. *Lipids serve as carriers for the fat-soluble vitamins—A, D, E and K.*

Fats are also involved in many different chemical processes in the body. Fatty layers under the skin serve as an insulator against heat loss. An important component of lipids are the fatty acids. The alpha-linolenate acids are three fatty acids—oleic, linoleic and linolenic—that cannot be manufactured by the cat's body and must be supplied by food. They are necessary for normal growth, healthy blood, arteries and nerves, normal kidney function and they keep the skin and hair coat healthy and supple.

Fats are also the primary source of energy for your cat. *Fats furnish more than twice the number of calories (or energy) per gram than do carbohydrates or protein.*

Too much fat can lead to obesity and its associated problems. Excessive fat intake will also slow down digestion, resulting in nausea, diarrhea and sometimes, vomiting. A fat deficiency will often show up as dry, flaky skin and dull hair coat. An extreme deficiency in a young cat will lead to slow growth. A rare fatty acid deficiency may show up as liver disease, pancreatitus or chronic digestive disorders.

SOURCES OF FATS. Animal fats are one source of fat, and many cat food manufacturers add animal fat to their foods, both to increase palatability and for the fat itself. However, the high temperatures used to process foods can eliminate the fatty acid content of the food and destroy part of its effectiveness to the cat.

Some cat food manufacturers add a cold-pressed oil—such as linseed, wheat germ or soybean—to supply the needed lipids. Ideally, the cat food should contain animal fat and a cold-pressed oil and the label should list all three of the fatty acids—oleic acid, linolenic acid and linoleic acid.

FIBER: THE "ACTION" BUILDING BLOCK

Fiber is the part of food that is not digested by the cat's body, such as cellulose. Just because it is not digested doesn't mean it's worthless or wasted food, though. Fiber is necessary for good intestinal health by absorbing water and aiding in the formation and movement of feces.

Low-calorie diets for overweight cats normally have an increased amount of fiber because the cat can then eat a good amount of food, feel full and yet be consuming fewer calories.

BALANCING NUTRIENTS

All of these nutrients work together, as do the other building blocks mentioned in the next chapter. Even though protein is one of the most important nutrients a cat can eat, a diet of pure protein will not sustain life over a long-term period and certainly will not allow for healthy reproduction.

Each individual cat has its own dietary needs for protein, fat, carbohydrates and fiber, as well as the other nutrient building blocks.

CHART 2
PRIMARY BUILDING BLOCK COMPARISONS:
KITTEN GROWTH FOODS

Company/Brand	% Protein	% Fat	% Fiber	% Moisture
Friskies				
Kitten Turkey canned	12	6.5	1	78
Mixed Grill canned	12	5	1	78
Ocean Whitefish canned	14	3	1	78
Friskies Kitten dry	35	9	4	10
Hill's				
Science Diet Growth				
canned	13	8	1	72
Growth dry	33	23	3	10
Nutro Max				
Kitten dry	34	20	3	10
Purina				
Kitten Chow Dairy dry	35	8.5	4	12
Sensible Choice				
Kitten Chicken and				
Rice dry	33	20	3	10
Vet's Choice Select Balance				
Kitten canned	13	8	1	72
Vet's Choice Select Care				
Kitten canned	10.6	7.1	0.3	NL*
Kitten dry	34.4	20.4	1.1	NL
Waltham Growth				
Chicken canned	11	7.5	1	78

Note: To convert foods to a dry matter basis so that they can be compared equally, see Chart 13.
* NL stands for Not Listed.

CHART 3
PRIMARY BUILDING BLOCK COMPARISONS:
ADULT/MAINTENANCE FOODS

Company/Brand	% Protein	% Fat	% Fiber	% Moisture
Alpo				
Seafood Flavor dry	30	8	4	12
Tuna canned	18	2	1	78
Grill canned	11	4.5	1	78
Aristocrat				
Whitefish and Tuna				
canned	10	5	1	78
Chicken Slices canned	8	2	1	82
Breeder's Choice				
Avo-cat Oceanfish				
canned	10	7	1	78
Beef canned	10	7	1	78
Chicken canned	10	7	1	78
Century Pet Care				
Carnivore dry	32	18	3	10
Friskies Fancy Feast				
Beef and Chicken				
canned	10.5	6	1	78
Oceanfish canned	11	2	1	78
Whitefish canned	13	2	1	78
Tender Beef canned	11	4	1	78
Heinz 9 Lives				
Plus Turkey and Rice				
canned	9	5.5	1	78
Tuna and Cheese				
canned	15.5	2	1	78
Hill's Science Diet				
Feline Maintenance dry	30	20	2	10

Company/Brand	% Protein	% Fat	% Fiber	% Moisture
Iams				
Lamb and Rice dry	32	21	3	10
Oceanfish canned	10	6.5	1	78
Catfish canned	10	6.5	1	78
Lamb and Rice canned	10	6.5	1	78
Beef canned	10	6.5	1	78
Cat Food dry	32	21	3	10
Innova				
dry	36	20	2.5	10
Kal Kan				
Whiskas canned	9	5	1.5	78
Optimum Beef canned	8	5	1.5	78
Optimum Seafood canned	8	5	1.5	78
Optimum Chicken canned	8	5	1.5	78
Nature's Recipe				
Optimum Chicken canned	10	6	1.5	78
Optimum Beef canned	11	5	1	78
Nutro Max				
Adult Ocean Fish canned	10	5	1	78
Nutro Natural Choice				
Chicken, Lamb and Rice canned	10	5	1	78
Old Mother Hubbard				
Neura Cat Food dry	30	18	2	11

CHART 3, Continued

Company/Brand	% Protein	% Fat	% Fiber	% Moisture
Purina				
Cat Chow dry	31.5	8	4.5	12
Kit 'N Kaboodle dry	30	8	4.5	12
ONE dry	31	12.5	2	10
Ocean Whitefish				
canned	11.5	4.2	1	78
Rainbow Trout				
canned	11.5	4.5	1	78
Country Dinner				
canned	11	3	1	78
Sensible Choice				
Chicken and Rice dry	30	15	3	10
Vet's Choice				
Select Balance canned	11.5	6.5	1	72
Wal-Mart				
Special Kitty dry	31.5	9	4	12

Note: When comparing dry and canned foods, convert all foods to a dry matter basis. For the formula, see Chart 13.

CHART 4
PRIMARY BUILDING BLOCK COMPARISONS:
LESS ACTIVE/REDUCING FOODS

Company/Brand	% Protein	% Fat	% Fiber	% Moisture
Hill's Science Diet				
Maintenance Lite				
canned	10	3	2.5	78
Iams Less Active				
Fish and Rice canned	10	3.5	1	78
Chicken and Rice canned	10	3.5	1	78
Less Active for Cats dry	28	14	3	10
Nutro Max Lite				
canned	10	5	1	78
Vet's Choice Select Balance				
Less Active canned	10	3	2.5	78
Vet's Choice Select Care				
HiFiber Formula dry	32.9	9.3	7.8	NL*
HiFiber Formula canned	8.4	3	2.1	NL
Waltham				
Lite Chicken canned	8	4	2.5	84

Note: To compare these and other foods on an equal basis, convert all foods to a dry matter basis. See Chart 13.
*NL stands for Not Listed.

CHART 5
PRIMARY BUILDING BLOCK COMPARISONS:
SENIOR, GERIATRIC AND SPECIAL FOODS

Company/Brand	% Protein	% Fat	% Fiber	% Moisture
Friskies				
Special Diet Turkey canned	10	6.5	0.5	78
Special Diet Ocean canned	10	6.5	0.5	78
Senior Beef canned	9	3	1	82
Nutro Max Lite				
dry	32	10	6	10
Purina				
Cat Chow Special Care dry	31	13	2.5	10
Vet's Choice Select Care				
Control Formula dry	31.4	21.5	1.2	NL*
Control Formula canned	10.6	7.1	0.2	NL
Mature Formula dry	27.2	15.6	2	NL
Mature Formula canned	9.1	15.6	2	NL
Waltham				
Senior Diet canned	8	6	2	78

Note: To compare foods on an equal basis, convert these and all foods to a dry matter basis. See Chart 13.
*NL stands for Not Listed.

CHART 6
SECONDARY BUILDING BLOCK COMPARISONS: KITTEN GROWTH FOODS

Company/Brand	% Ash	% Cal	% Phos	% Mag	% Tau
Friskies Kitten					
dry	NL*	1.5	1.2	NL	.1
Hill's Science Diet					
Growth dry	6.5	.9	.7	.11	.1
Growth canned	2.5	.3	.25	.04	NL
Nutro Max					
Kitten dry	7	NL	NL	NL	NL
Purina					
Kitten Dairy dry	NL	1.1	.9	NL	.125
Sensible Choice					
Kitten Chicken					
and Rice dry	6	NL	NL	.09	NL
Vet's Choice Select Balance					
Kitten canned	2.5	.3	.23	.04	.056
Vet's Choice Select Care					
Kitten dry	6.6	1.28	.97	.086	NL

*NL stands for Not Listed.

CHART 7
SECONDARY BUILDING BLOCK COMPARISONS:
ADULT/MAINTENANCE FOODS

Company/Brand	% Ash	% Cal	% Phos	% Mag	% Tau
Alpo					
Tuna canned	3.5	NL*	NL	.04	.05
Grill canned	2.5	NL	NL	.03	.05
Seafood dry	NL	1	0.9	NL	NL
Aristocrat					
Whitefish					
canned	3.5	NL	NL	NL	.05
Chicken Slices					
canned	2.5	NL	NL	NL	.05
Avo-cat Breeder's Choice					
Chicken canned	1.5	NL	NL	.04	.05
Beef canned	1.5	NL	NL	.04	.05
Century Pet Care					
Carnivore dry	6.5	NL	NL	0.1	0.1
Friskies Fancy Feast					
Beef and Chicken					
canned	2.8	NL	NL	NL	.05
Oceanfish					
canned	2.7	NL	NL	NL	.05
Whitefish					
canned	3.7	NL	NL	NL	.05
Tender Beef					
canned	3.5	NL	NL	NL	.05
Heinz 9 Lives Plus					
Turkey and Rice					
canned	4.0	NL	NL	NL	.05
Tuna and Cheese					
canned	4.0	NL	NL	NL	.05

Company/Brand	% Ash	% Cal	% Phos	% Mag	% Tau
Hill's Science Diet					
Maintenance dry	5.0	0.6	0.5	0.1	0.1
Iams					
Lamb and Rice dry	7	NL	NL	0.1	NL
Innova					
dry	6	NL	NL	0.1	NL
Nutro Max Adult					
Oceanfish					
canned	2.5	NL	NL	.022	.05
Nutro Natural Choice					
Chicken, lamb					
canned	2.5	NL	NL	.022	.05
Old Mother Hubbard					
Neura dry	5	0.8	0.6	0.1	NL
Purina					
Oceanfish					
canned	3	NL	NL	NL	.055
Rainbow Trout					
canned	4	NL	NL	NL	.055
Country Dinner					
canned	4	NL	NL	NL	.055
Cat Chow dry	NL	1.2	1	NL	.125
Kit 'N Kaboodle					
dry	NL	1	0.8	1.5	NL
ONE dry	5.5	0.8	0.7	.08	.15
Sensible Choice					
Chicken and Rice					
dry	NL	NL	NL	NL	NL

CHART 7, CONTINUED

Company/Brand	% Ash	% Cal	% Phos	% Mag	% Tau
Vet's Choice Select Balance					
Adult Cat can	1.9	0.2	.15	.025	.056
Wal-Mart					
Special Kitty dry	NL	1	0.8	NL	.125

* NL stands for Not Listed.

CHART 8
SECONDARY BUILDING BLOCK COMPARISONS:
GERIATRIC, REDUCING AND SPECIAL DIETS

Company/Brand	% Ash	% Cal	% Phos	% Mag	% Tau
Friskies Special Diet					
Oceanfish					
canned	2.8	NL*	NL	.024	.05
Turkey canned	2.8	NL	NL	.024	.05
Friskies Senior					
Beef canned	2	NL	NL	NL	.05
Hill's Science Diet					
Maintenance Lite					
canned	1.9	.15	.1	.024	.05
Iams Less Active					
Fish, Rice					
canned	1.9	NL	NL	.025	NL
Chicken, Rice					
canned	1.9	NL	NL	.03	NL
Nutro					
Max Lite dry	6.5	NL	NL	.1	NL
Max Lite can	1.9	NL	NL	.022	.05
Purina Cat Chow					
Special Care dry	6	NL	NL	.08	.125
Vet's Choice Select Balance					
Less Active					
canned	1.9	.15	.11	.024	.044
Waltham Senior					
Chicken canned	2	NL	NL	.03	.05
Waltham Lite					
Chicken canned	2	NL	NL	.025	.05

* NL stands for Not Listed.

FOUR

THE OTHER BUILDING BLOCKS: VITAMINS AND MINERALS

The discovery of vitamins in 1910 was one of the most exciting achievements in the field of nutrition. Prior to their discovery, researchers knew that substances were needed for good health, but those substances were unknown. Although nutritionists and researchers have learned much about vitamins since their discovery, experts readily admit there is still much that is unknown, including the amounts of many vitamins needed for good health.

For example, in 1970 Linus Pauling created havoc in the nutritional and medical fields when his experiments showed that massive doses of vitamin C could prevent or cure many diseases. Research is still continuing and is constantly producing therapeutic applications for vitamins.

WHAT ARE VITAMINS AND WHAT DO THEY DO?

Vitamins are organic substances found only in plants or animals. With a few exceptions, the cat's body cannot synthesize vitamins; therefore, vitamins must be supplied in food or in supplements.

In your cat's body, vitamins function together and with enzymes and have a variety of different functions including:

- digestion
- metabolism
- growth
- reproduction

• cellular reproduction

• oxidation

Vitamins are required for tens of thousands of different chemical actions. Because vitamins work on a cellular level, a vitamin toxicity or deficiency can have a number of different, potentially lethal, repercussions. The levels required for toxicity or deficiency can vary between cats, making it even harder to decide what your cat should get.

SHOULD YOU SUPPLEMENT?

Deciding what vitamins your cat should get and how much is very difficult, even for researchers. Some researchers feel that a diet of natural foods contains adequate amounts of vitamins and minerals; that over supplementation can destroy the nutritional balance of the food and even be hazardous to the animal's health. Other researchers believe that a certain amount of supplementation is needed for several reasons, the most important being that a commercial diet is not a natural diet. A cat in the wild is not eating a diet of cooked meat and processed grains; it is eating wild rodents and birds that eat a variety of things, which in turn the cat absorbs when it eats the prey. Before you decide whether or not to add a vitamin supplement to your cat's food, there is a lot more you need to know. First, you need to understand vitamins and minerals and how they affect your cat's health. We'll discuss the various commercial foods and their quality, and then we will discuss supplements themselves in Chapter Eight.

INDIVIDUAL VITAMINS EXPLAINED

VITAMIN A. Vitamin A is a fat soluble vitamin which has two forms: *carotene* and *vitamin A*. Carotene must be converted into vitamin A before it can be used by the body. Preformed vitamin A is the result of that chemical conversion. As a fat-soluble vitamin, excess vitamin A is stored in the liver, in fat tissues, lungs, kidneys and retinas of the eyes.

Vitamin A is an important antioxidant and helps in growth and the repair of body tissues, aids in digestion and protects mucus membranes, aiding in disease resistance. An immune system enhancing substance, vitamin A is also necessary for building strong bones, teeth and claws, as well as healthy blood. Vitamin A is also responsible for good eyesight.

A vitamin A deficiency will cause slow or retarded growth, reproductive failure and skin disorders. Secondary infections are also common, as are eye disorders. Because vitamin A is a fat-soluble vitamin, if too much is ingested, it can be toxic. Too much vitamin A has also been associated with bone deformities, joint pain and bleeding.

Vitamin A can be found in green leafy vegetables, such as spinach and broccoli. It is also found in fish oils and animal liver. Most commercial cat food and supplement manufacturers add vitamin A in one form or another to the food or supplement rather than counting on the ingredients to retain the vitamin during processing.

THE B VITAMINS. There are a variety of B vitamins. This group is often called the vitamin B complex and includes B1 (thiamine), B2 (riboflavin), B3 (niacin), B5 (pantothenic acid), B6 (pyridoxine), B12 (cyanocobalamin) and B15 (pangamic acid). The B complex also includes biotin, choline, folic acid, inositol and para-aminobenzoic acid (PABA).

The B-complex vitamins help provide energy by assisting in the conversion of carbohydrates to glucose, which in turn is the body's fuel. The B vitamins are also help metabolize protein and fat. These vitamins are needed for normal functioning of the nervous system, for good muscle tone and for healthy skin.

Vitamin B1 (thiamine) works with enzymes to help convert glucose to energy. Also known as the "morale" vitamin, thiamine also works with the nervous system and is beneficial to a good mental attitude. Although it is known to improve individual learning capacity in children, this has not yet been proven in animals.

Vitamin B2 (riboflavin) assists in the chemical breakdown of foods. It also works with enzymes to help cells utilize oxygen. Riboflavin is also needed for good vision, healthy skin and nails.

Vitamin B3 (niacin) works with enzymes to metabolize food. It is also effective in improving circulation, reducing cholesterol and is important in maintaining a healthy nervous system.

Vitamin B5 (pantothenic acid) stimulates the adrenal glands, which increases production of adrenal hormones necessary for good health. Vitamin B5 aids digestion, is good for healthy skin and hair coat and also helps the body withstand stress better. **Vitamin B6** (pyridoxine) is necessary for absorption of vitamin B12. It also helps linoleic acids function better in the cat's body. B6 is also needed for the production of red blood cells and antibodies.

Vitamin B12 (cyanocobalamin) is a cobalt containing vitamin that works with enzymes to assist in normal DNA synthesis. B12 also works with the nervous system, appetite and food metabolism.

Vitamin B15 (pangamic acid) works to eliminate hypoxia (oxygen insufficiency) in body tissues, especially muscles. B15 also stimulates the glandular systems.

The other B complex vitamins also serve vital functions. **Biotin** assists in the oxidation of fatty acids and in the metabolism of other foods. Biotin is also required by the other B vitamins for metabolism.

Choline functions with inositol as a basic ingredient of lecithin.

Folic acid works with B12 and C to metabolize proteins. Folic acid is also necessary for the formation of red blood cells.

All of these B vitamins are water soluble and as a result, excess vitamins are excreted instead of being stored in the body. Because the vitamins are not retained, they must be replenished in the diet. The B complex vitamins are found primarily in brewer's yeast, liver and whole grain cereals.

Sulfa drugs, insecticides and estrogen can destroy these vitamins in the digestive tract. It is also important to remember that most of the B vitamins work together and if given as a supplement, should be given together. An excess of one B vitamin could cause a deficiency (or excess) of another.

VITAMIN C. Vitamin C has caused more uproar than any other vitamin available. In humans, vitamin C has been labeled a "miracle" vitamin because of its ability to fight the common cold. It also serves as an aid in the formation of red bloods cells. Vitamin C also fights bacterial infections, maintains collagen, helps to heal wounds and prevents some hemorrhaging. Most importantly, vitamin C is known to help boost the immune system, fighting and killing viruses.

However, even though vitamin C has so many beneficial properties, many researchers do not feel that supplementing vitamin C to cats is needed. Most cats are able to synthesize Vitamin C internally and these researchers feel that any additional vitamin C would be wasted. Some researchers also feel that excess vitamin C can cause a change in the pH balance in the kidneys.

However, many other researchers believe otherwise. Alfred Plechner, DVM, stated in his book, *Pet Allergies: Remedies for an Epidemic*, "I do believe in vitamin C. It can indeed be helpful in many ways for many animals. Among other things, vitamin C contributes directly to adrenal health and function." Other experts feel vitamin C can help prevent orthopedic problems in fast growing kittens.

As the debate continues, many cat food manufacturers are adding vitamin C to their foods, sometimes using ascorbic acid as a preservative. Granted, the amount used to preserve food is small, has a short shelf life and is usually mixed with other substances; however, it is a vitamin C supplement.

At this point, research (and debate) is ongoing, and until some definitive answers are found it will be up to the individual cat owner as to whether or not to supplement vitamin C.

VITAMIN D. Known as the sunshine vitamin, vitamin D can be acquired from food or it can be absorbed from exposure to the sun. Vitamin D is needed for normal calcium–phosphorus metabolism by aiding in the absorption of calcium in the intestinal tract and the assimilation of phosphorus. Vitamin D is needed for normal growth, healthy bones and teeth.

Vitamin D works in conjunction with vitamin A, and a deficiency of vitamin A or D can lead to rickets and other bone diseases and deformities. It can also lead to vision problems and kidney disease. Vitamin D is a fat-soluble vitamin and excess is stored in the liver, brain and skin. Too much can lead to excess calcium and phosphorus in the system, causing calcification in the blood vessels, soft tissues and kidneys.

VITAMIN E. Vitamin E, a fat-soluble vitamin, is actually a group of substances called *tocopherols*. Found in cold-pressed vegetable oils, raw seeds, nuts and soybeans, tocopherols are antioxidants; substances that oppose oxidation in the cat's body. Fat oxidation results in free radicals that can cause extensive damage to the cat's body. Vitamin E protects both the pituitary and adrenal hormones from oxidation, as well as vitamin B complex and vitamin C.

Vitamin E also assists in the cellular respiration of muscle tissue, including the heart. It also dilates the blood vessels, allowing more blood to reach the heart, and it works to prevent blood clots from forming in blood vessels.

Many cat food manufacturers add vitamin E to their foods, often using tocopherols and ascorbic acids as preservatives.

VITAMIN K. Vitamin K is necessary for blood clotting and for normal liver functions. A fat-soluble vitamin, toxicity and abnormal blood clotting can result from too high a dosage.

The best sources of vitamin K are green leafy vegetables, milk, yogurt, eggs and fish oils.

ALL ABOUT MINERALS

Minerals are present, to some extent, in the tissues of all living things. Minerals make up parts of your cat's bones, teeth, muscles, blood and nerves. Minerals help keep the bones strong and the nerves healthy and reactive.

Minerals work with vitamins, with enzymes and with each other. For example, calcium and phosphorus are so closely related and their functions are so intertwined, they could actually be called one mineral; calcium-phosphorus. But they are really two minerals that function best together. Many other vitamins and minerals work the same way. The B-complex vitamins also need phosphorus for best metabolism; iron needs vitamin C for best absorption and zinc helps vitamin A to be released from the liver. A deficiency in any one mineral can have drastic effects on many systems in the body.

INDIVIDUAL MINERALS EXPLAINED

CALCIUM AND PHOSPHORUS. As was just mentioned, calcium and phosphorus are two separate minerals but their functions are so closely intertwined, they could almost be referred to as one combined mineral. Calcium is needed for muscle contraction and neuromuscular transmission and for blood coagulation. Calcium is also vital to some of the body's enzyme reactions.

Because it is present in every cell, phosphorus plays a part in almost every chemical reaction in the body. It is part of the digestion process, and in the production of energy it helps stimulate muscle contractions, including the heart muscle. It is also a vital part of cell reproduction. Working together, calcium and phosphorus' most important function is to strengthen bones and teeth. However, too much phosphorus will inhibit calcium metabolism, resulting in calcium deficiencies.

A calcium deficiency can cause rickets and bone and skeletal disorders and malformations. Moderate deficiencies may cause muscular cramps, joint pain, slow pulse and impaired growth.

Meat contains good quantities of phosphorus; while milk and milk products have both phosphorus and calcium. Many commercial cat foods have among their ingredients bone meal or calcium carbonate, either of which is a good source of these nutrients.

CHLORIDE. Chloride is found throughout the body and helps regulate the correct balance of acid and alkali in the blood. Working with salts, chloride maintains pressure in the cells that allows fluids to pass in and out of cell membranes. It is also needed by the liver to filter wastes from the system.

A deficiency is usually rare as chloride is found in table salt and most diets contain adequate amounts of salt. However, a deficiency of chloride can cause impaired digestion and poor muscular contraction.

COPPER. Copper assists in the absorption of iron, which is required for hemoglobin synthesis. Copper is also involved in the healing process and helps oxidize vitamin C. Copper is needed to build strong bones, to synthesize phospholipids and to form elastin.

A copper deficiency results in a type of anemia, much like that caused by an iron deficiency. A deficiency can also cause bone or skeletal abnormalities.

Copper is found in liver and fish, as well as whole grains and legumes. The amount of copper found in plant sources can vary depending upon the richness of the mineral in the soil where they were grown.

IODINE. Iodine is a trace mineral that is vital to the proper functioning of the thyroid gland. It plays an important part in regulating the body's energy, in promoting growth and in stimulating the rate of metabolism.

A deficiency of iodine can cause hypothyroidism (an abnormally low secretion of the thyroid hormones), obesity, sluggishness, nervousness and irritability.

Iodine is found in fish, as well as salt with iodine added. Many commercial cat foods add iodine or potassium iodide as a supplement.

IRON. Iron, working with protein, is present in every living cell in the body. The primary function of iron is to combine with protein and copper to make hemoglobin, which transports oxygen. Iron also works with enzymes to promote protein metabolism. Besides proteins and copper, iron needs calcium to work properly.

A deficiency of iron can cause anemia, the symptoms of which can include difficulty breathing and constipation.

Iron is found in liver, lean meats and fish. Leafy green vegetables, whole grains and legumes also contain iron.

MAGNESIUM. Magnesium helps promote the absorption and metabolism of vitamins and other minerals, including vitamins C and E, calcium, phosphorus, sodium and potassium. Magnesium is also important to protein and carbohydrate metabolism. It aids bone growth, and in fact, over 70 percent of all magnesium is located in the bones. A deficiency of magnesium will cause cardiac irregularities, muscle twitch and tremors and depression.

Magnesium can be found in leafy green vegetables, raw wheat germ and other whole grains, soybeans, milk, fish and oil-rich nuts and seeds. It is important to keep in mind that cooking, especially at high temperatures, removes magnesium from food, EXCEPT that food processed at very high temperatures and burned, creates ash, of which magnesium is a component.

ZINC. Zinc is a trace element with a number of important functions; it is vital for the metabolism of a number of vitamins, including the B-complex vitamins. Zinc is also a part of many different enzymes necessary for digestion and metabolism. Zinc is also needed for the healing processes.

Too much calcium in the diet can hamper the absorption of zinc, as can a diet too high in cellulose. A deficiency will show up as a delayed sexual maturity, slow or retarded growth or diabetes.

OTHER MINERALS. There are several other minerals important to your cat's good health. Selenium works with an enzyme and vitamin E to protect cells. Selenium is found in both meats and cereals and a deficiency is rare. Manganese, too, works with enzymes and is important to bone growth and reproduction. Cobalt, sulfur and fluorine are other minerals included in your cat's diet.

MAINTAINING A BALANCE

When discussing your cat's vitamin and mineral needs, it's important to keep in mind that no one vitamin or mineral functions alone; each has its own function and place in the system but each is also dependent upon the others. Even if you or your veterinarian decide that your cat has a deficiency, you must remember to keep the balance of all the nutrients when you supplement your pet's diet.

WHAT'S ALL THE FUSS ABOUT TAURINE?

Taurine is an amino acid that has many effects on the body. Taurine works with the electrically active tissues, such as the brain and heart, to help stabilize cell membranes. Taurine aids in the movement of magnesium, calcium, sodium and potassium in and out of cells, again, generating nerve impulses. Taurine has been used to treat seizure disorders, heart disease, hypertension and high cholesterol.

Several years ago veterinarians were seeing several health problems that were eventually traced to low levels of taurine in commercial cat food. Heart problems were prevalent as well as vision problems, depression, cirrhosis and low reproduction. At the time, most of the commercial cat food companies were including taurine in their foods at several times the levels recommended by the National Research Council, but for some unknown reason, the cats were not metabolizing the taurine in the food.

Today, almost all cat food manufacturers fortify their cat food formulas with a more digestible form of taurine. Deficiencies are still seen, though, for several different reasons. A disease called aminoaciduria causes the taurine to be excreted in the cat's urine. Some cats simply do not absorb the amino acid properly, and cats fed a diet that is not balanced with all nutrients can suffer a deficiency.

If you feel that your cat may be suffering from a taurine deficiency, talk to your veterinarian. He may recommend another cat food or possibly a taurine supplement. If you have questions about the taurine in your cat's food, call the manufacturer.

CHART 9
SOURCES OF VITAMINS

Vitamin	Most Common Source
Vitamin A	Dairy products, leafy green vegetables, fish liver oil, carrots
Vitamin B Complex	Brewer's yeast, whole grain cereals, liver
Vitamin C	Fruits and vegetables, especially broccoli, cabbage, leafy green vegetables
Vitamin D	Sunshine. Dairy products, fish liver oil
Vitamin E	Cold-pressed vegetable oil, meats, raw nuts and seeds, leafy green vegetables, soybeans
Vitamin K	Kelp, alfalfa, yogurt, egg yolks, fish liver oils

CHART 10
VITAMIN DEFICIENCIES AND EXCESSES

Vitamin A

Deficiency: Vision problems, slow growth, skin and coat problems, diarrhea.

Excess: Nausea, vomiting, diarrhea, hair coat loss, bone deformities, bleeding disorders.

Vitamin B Complex

Deficiency: Fatigue, irritability, nervousness, hair coat loss, skin problems.

Excess: Water soluble; when taken as a complex, excess is usually excreted in the urine. Unusual excess can cause nerve damage, blood or digestive disorders.

Vitamin C (Research ongoing and greatly debated)

Deficiency: Impaired lactation, shortness of breath, swollen joints, slow healing, poor dental condition.

Excess: Water soluble; most excess excreted in the urine. High doses can result in diarrhea.

CHART 10, Continued

Vitamin D

Deficiency: Rickets, bone deformities, poorly developed muscles, nervous disorders, vision problems.

Excess: Increased frequency of urination, nausea, vomiting, muscular weakness, calcification of muscles, including the heart.

Vitamin E

Deficiency: Blood and bleeding disorders, collagen problems, a break down in amino acids, reduction in functioning of several hormones, reproductive failure.

Excess: Generally considered nontoxic, however, it can cause elevated blood pressure.

Vitamin K

Deficiency: Bleeding disorders, miscarriage.

Excess: Generally considered nontoxic.

CHART 11
SOURCES OF MINERALS

Mineral	Most Common Source
Calcium	Meats, bone and bone meal, milk and milk products
Chloride	Salt (sodium chloride), kelp
Copper	Liver, whole grain products, leafy green vegetables, legumes
Iodine	Fish, kelp
Iron	Liver, oysters, fish, lean meats, leafy green vegetables, whole grains, legumes, molasses
Magnesium	Green vegetables, raw, whole grains, oil-rich seeds and nuts, soybeans, milk
Manganese	Whole grains, eggs, seeds and nuts, green vegetables
Phosphorus	Meat, fish, poultry, eggs, whole grains, seeds and nuts

Potassium	All vegetables, potatoes, bananas, whole grains, sunflower seeds
Selenium	Yeast, organ and muscle meats, fish, whole grains.
Sulfur	Eggs, meat, cheese
Zinc	Whole grains, brewer's yeast, wheat germ, pumpkin seeds

CHART 12
MINERAL DEFICIENCIES AND EXCESSES

Calcium/Phosphorus
Deficiency: Rickets, bone deformities, slow growth, irritability, depression.
Excess: Must have balance between both minerals.

Chloride
Deficiency: Hair coat loss, impaired digestion, poor muscular contractions.
Excess: Adverse reactions suspected but unknown.

Copper
Deficiency: General weakness, impaired respiration, anemia, skeletal abnormalities, skin sores.
Excess: Toxic hepatitis.

Iodine
Deficiency: Enlarged thyroid, dry skin and hair coat, loss of vigor, slow/poor growth, reproductive failure.
Excess: Unknown.

Iron
Deficiency: Weak, constipation, anemia.
Excess: Unknown.

Magnesium
Deficiency: Neuromuscular excitability or irritability, tremors, depression.
Excess: Can lead to Feline Urological Syndrome (FUS).

CHART 12, CONTINUED

Manganese

Deficiency: Slow or retarded growth, reproductive failure, abnormal bone growth, paralysis, ataxia, blindness, deafness.

Excess: Unknown.

Potassium

Deficiency: Respiratory failure, cardiac arrest, nervous disorders, insomnia.

Excess: Unknown.

Selenium

Deficiency: Premature aging, kitten death, skeletal and cardiac myopathies.

Excess: Hepatitis, nephritis.

Sulfur

Deficiency: Slow or retarded growth, sluggishness, fatigue.

Excess: Unknown.

Zinc

Deficiency: Retarded growth, delayed sexual maturity, diabetes, skin problems.

Excess: Relatively nontoxic but excessive intake may have harmful side effects.

FIVE

UNDERSTANDING CAT FOOD AND CAT FOOD LABELS

In previous chapters we discussed your cat's nutritional needs: proteins for energy, for building healthy cells and for growth; fats for processing vitamins and keeping skin and coat healthy; carbohydrates and fiber for energy and digestibility and, of course, plenty of clean water. We know that vitamins and minerals often work together and with enzymes for cell function and growth. We even know what foods contain these nutritional building blocks. But how do we know whether a commercial food is supplying these needs?

Unfortunately, there is no easy answer. In fact the nutritional needs of cats (and dogs) and the quality of commercial cat (and dog) foods are two highly debated subjects—ones that have some researchers fervently defending one position and others arguing exactly the opposite.

Alfred Plechner, DVM, author of *Pet Allergies: Remedies for an Epidemic* (Very Healthy Enterprises, 1986), states in his book, "I discovered that many commercial food formulations are woefully deficient in key nutrients." He continues by condemning the quality of ingredients used by many pet food manufacturers—the moldy grains, rancid foods and meat meal made from slaughterhouse discards.

However, pet food companies emphasize the quality of their foods and point to the generations of dogs and cats residing in their care centers, eating the food the company produces and looking the picture of health.

In this chapter, we will discuss both sides of the various issues as thoroughly as possible. Ultimately, it's up to you as the cat owner and consumer to decide what you want your cat to eat.

DISSECTING THE CAT FOOD LABEL

Every cat food label must include specific information, which is usually divided into two parts: the principal display panel and the information panel.

The **principal display panel** is very straightforward. It provides the food's:

1. brand name (Iams, Purina, Friskies, etc.)
2. identity statement (describes the contents: Beef Dinner, Ocean Whitefish, etc.)
3. designator (identifies the species and growth stage: for kittens, for senior cats, etc.)
4. quantity of contents (identifies the weight of the contents)

The **information panel** provides the food's:

1. guaranteed analysis (shows the "as is" percentages of the foods contents)
2. ingredients list (shows the ingredients, in descending order, by weight)
3. nutritional adequacy claim (identifies specific life stage and whether feeding tests were conducted based on AAFCO procedures)
4. feeding instructions (how much food to feed)

The principal display panel is like the name of your town: It identifies where you are, but it doesn't tell you how to get around. For a "road map" of the food, you need to be able to "read" the stuff on the information panel. Let's review the first three items found there.

GUARANTEED ANALYSIS

The guaranteed analysis on the information panel of the cat food label lists the minimum levels of crude protein and fat and the maximum levels of fiber and water. Most labels also list the maximum levels of ash and/or magnesium and some list sodium. The term "crude" refers to the total content, not necessarily the amount that is actually digestible. Therefore, crude protein and fat amounts are simply rough guides. The actual amount depends upon the ingredients and their quality.

The amount of moisture in a food is important, especially when you are comparing foods. A food containing 24 percent protein and 10 percent moisture would have less protein per serving than a food with the same percentage of protein listed on the label but with only 6 percent moisture. To compare foods, convert the percentages to a dry matter basis (See Chart 13).

The guaranteed analysis is only a starting place to read when looking at the label because it contains so little information. Hill's Pet Products, makers of Science Diet foods, used an advertisement in 1984 that was an excellent demonstration of how the guaranteed analysis could fool the unsuspecting food buyer. The ad listed a guaranteed analysis, just like one from a can of dog food, and listed crude protein at 10 percent, fat at 6.5 percent, fiber at 2.4 percent and moisture at 68 percent. Typical numbers for canned food. However, the list of ingredients was a shocker. Four pairs of old leather work shoes, one gallon of used crankcase oil, one pail of crushed coal, and 68 pounds of water. These ingredients, when analyzed, would equal the guaranteed analysis. Not very nourishing for the dog!

INGREDIENT LIST

Ingredients are listed in descending order, by weight. However, the listing may be misleading. Suppose you see beef is the first ingredient listed. You would then assume that beef is the primary ingredient. Look again. If it's followed by wheat flour, wheat germ and wheat middlings, the combined wheat products may very well total much more than the total amount of beef.

The following is a list of some of the ingredients found in commercial cat foods. These descriptions are based on the definitions for animal feed established by the Association of American Feed Control Officials (AAFCO).

MEAT OR MEAT BASED INGREDIENTS

Meat is the clean flesh of slaughtered cattle, swine, sheep or goats. It may be only striated skeletal muscle, tongue, diaphragm, heart or esophagus, overlying fat and the portions of skin, sinew, nerve and blood vessels normally found with that flesh.

Meat By-Products are the clean parts of slaughtered animals; not including meat. It does include lungs, spleen, kidneys, brain, livers, blood, bone, partially defatted low temperature fatty tissue, and stomachs and intestines freed of their contents. It does not include hair, horns, teeth or hooves.

Meat Meal is rendered meal made from animal tissues. It cannot contain blood, hair, hoof, horn, hide trimmings, manure, stomach or rumen contents, except for amounts which may be unavoidably included during processing. It cannot contain any added extraneous materials and may not contain any more than 14 percent indigestible materials, and not more than 11 percent of the crude protein in the meal may be indigestible by the cat.

Meat and Bone Meal is rendered from meat, including bone, but doesn't include blood, hair, hoof, horn, hide trimmings, manure, stomach and rumen contents, except small amounts unavoidably included during processing. It does not include any extraneous materials. Only 14 percent may be indigestible residue and no more than 11 percent of the crude protein may be indigestible.

Poultry By-Products are clean parts of slaughtered poultry, such as heads, feet, viscera and must not contain feces or foreign matter except in unavoidable trace amounts.

Poultry By-Product Meal consists of the ground, rendered, clean parts of slaughtered poultry, such as necks, feet, undeveloped eggs and intestines. It does not contain feathers, except those which are unavoidably included during processing.

Dehydrated Eggs are whole dried poultry eggs.

Animal By-Product Meal is made by rendering animal tissues which don't fit any of the other ingredient categories. It still cannot contain extra hair, hoof, horn, hide trimmings, manure, stomach or rumen contents, nor any extraneous material.

Animal Digest is a powder or liquid made by taking clean, un-decomposed animal tissue and breaking it down using chemical and/or enzymatic hydrolysis. It does not contain hair, horn, teeth, hooves or feathers, except in unavoidable trace amounts. Digest names must be descriptive of their contents: chicken digest must be made from chicken, beef from beef, and so on.

Beef Tallow is fat derived from beef.

Fish Meal is the clean, dried, ground tissue of undecomposed whole fish or fish cuttings, with or without the oil extracted.

PLANT, GRAIN AND OTHER INGREDIENTS

Alfalfa Meal is the finely ground product of the alfalfa plant.

Dried Whey is whey, dried, and is not less than 11 percent protein or less than 61 percent lactose.

Barley is at least 80 percent sound barley, no more than 3 percent heat damaged kernels, 6 percent foreign material, 20 percent other grains other grains or 10 percent wild oats.

Barley Flour is the soft, finely ground barley meal obtained from the milling of barley.

Beet Pulp is the dried residue from sugar production from sugar beets.

Ground Corn (also called corn meal or corn chop) is the entire corn kernel ground or chopped. It must contain no more than 4 percent foreign material.

Corn Gluten Meal is the by-product after the manufacture of corn syrup or starch; and is the dried residue after the removal of the bran, germ and starch and is high-quality protein.

Brewer's Rice is small fragments of rice kernels that have been separated from larger kernels of milled rice.

Brown Rice is the unpolished rice left over after the kernels have been removed.

Soybean Meal is a by-product of the production of soybean oil and is high in protein.

Ground Grain Sorghum is made by grinding the grains of grain sorghum.

Cereal Food Fines is a by-product of breakfast cereal production; particles of the foods.

Linseed Meal is the residue of flaxseed oil production, ground into a meal.

Peanut Hulls are the outer hull of the peanut shell, ground.

Dried Kelp is dried seaweed. The maximum percentage of salt and minimum percentage of potassium and iodine must be declared.

PRESERVATIVES

BHA and BHT are both preservatives. BHA is butylated hydroxyanisole. BHT is butylated hydroxytoluene. According to Dr. Alfred Plechner, both have been associated with liver damage, fetal abnormalities, metabolic stress and have, as Dr. Plechner states, "a questionable relationship to cancer."

Ethoxyquin has been the most highly debated item in dog and cat foods for the last several years. Ethoxyquin is a chemical preservative that has been widely used to prevent spoilage in pet foods. Ethoxyquin was approved by the FDA in 1956. It has been alleged that ethoxyquin has caused cancer, liver, kidney and thyroid dysfunctions, reproductive failure and more.

An independent testing laboratory is conducting a new test on ethoxyquin. This test is following testing protocols approved by the U.S. Food and Drug Administration (FDA). The FDA will evaluate the study prior to the results being released to the public.

Many pet food manufacturers still use ethoxyquin, however, because of public concern, many manufacturers have switched to other means of preserving their foods.

Sodium Nitrate is used both as a food coloring (red) and as a preservative. When used in food, sodium nitrate can produce carcinogenic substances called nitrosamines. Accidental ingestion of sodium nitrate by people can be fatal.

Tocopherols (vitamins C and E) are naturally occurring compounds used as natural preservatives. Tocopherols function as antioxidants, preventing the oxidation of fatty acids, vitamins and some other nutrients. These are being used more frequently as preservatives as many cat owners are more concerned about chemical preservatives. However, tocopherols have a very short shelf life, especially once the bag of food has been opened.

WHAT ARE THOSE OTHER INGREDIENTS?

The National Research Council believes that adequate amounts of needed nutrients can be obtained by eating a well-balanced diet consisting of a selection of the proper ingredients. However, Lavon J. Dunne, author of the *Nutrition Almanac* (Nutrition Search, Inc., McGraw Hill, 1990), states that there is much more to nutrition. "Other factors affecting adequate nutrition are insufficient soil nutrient levels resulting in nutrient deficient foods. Food processing and storage deplete foodstuffs of valuable vitamins and minerals." Dunne continues by saying that many nutrients are lost or depleted during cooking, especially at high temperatures.

When the label on the cat food states that the food is complete and balanced, that means the food contains all of the nutrients required by the Association of American Feed Control Officials (AAFCO). To satisfy those requirements, many cat food manufacturers add vitamins and minerals to the food during processing. Sometimes these are added in a natural form, as an ingredient. For example, yeast is added to many foods because it is an excellent source of selenium, chromium, iron, magnesium, manganese and many other needed nutrients.

Natural vitamins can be separated from their natural source, either plant or animal, and used as an additive. The vitamin (or mineral) is considered natural as long as there has been no change to the basic molecular structure.

The vitamins or minerals can also be added to the food in a synthetic, manufactured form. Synthetic vitamins and minerals usually contain a salt such as sulfate, nitrate or chloride, which helps stabilize the nutrient. Most researchers feel that the body absorbs synthetic vitamins as well as natural, with very little difference in metabolism, except for vitamin E, which works much better in natural form.

Many of the chemical names listed on cat food labels are the chemical names of natural or synthetic vitamins and minerals added to food during processing to ensure the food meets AAFCO requirements.

Ascorbic acid is a synthetic form of vitamin C.

Biotin is a natural B-complex vitamin.

Calcium carbonate is a natural form of calcium.

Calcium pantothenate is a high potency, synthetic source of vitamin B5.

Calcium oxide is a natural form of calcium.

Calcium phosphate is a calcium salt found in or derived from bones or bone meal.

Chloride or *chlorine* is an essential mineral, usually found in compound form with sodium or potassium.

Choline is a B vitamin found in eggs, liver and soy.

Choline chloride is a high potency, synthetic source of choline.

Cobalt is a trace element, an essential mineral and an integral part of vitamin B12.

Copper is a trace element, an essential mineral that can be toxic in excess.

Copper carbonate is a natural form of copper.

Copper gluconate is a synthetic form of copper.

Copper sulfate is a synthetic source of copper.

Ferrous sulfate is a high-potency, synthetic source of iron.

Folic acid is a B vitamin found in yeast or liver.

Inositol is a B-complex vitamin.

Iron oxide is a natural source of iron.

Magnesium oxide is a natural source of magnesium.

Menadione sodium bisulfite complex is a source for vitamin K activity.

Pangamic acid is vitamin B15.

Pantothenic acid is vitamin B5, a coenzyme.

Potassium chloride is a high potency, synthetic source of potassium.

Potassium citrate is a natural form of potassium.

Pyridoxine hydrochloride is a synthetic source of vitamin B6.

Riboflavin is a synthetic source of vitamin B2.

Selenium is an essential mineral.

Sodium chloride is a synthetic form of salt, table salt.

Sodium selenite is a synthetic form of the essential mineral, selenium.

Taurine is an amino acid.

Thiamine hydrochloride is a synthetic source of vitamin B1, thiamine.

Thiamine mononitrate is a synthetic source of vitamin B1.

Zinc carbonate is a source of the mineral zinc.

Zinc oxide is a natural form of the mineral zinc.

Zinc sulfate is a synthetic form of the mineral zinc.

ARTIFICIAL COLORING

Many of the artificial colorings used in cat foods have been associated with potential problems. FD&C Red No. 40 is a possible carcinogen but is widely used to keep the meat looking fresh. Blue No. 2 is thought to increase cats' sensitivity to viruses. Another color which is commonly used but has not been fully tested is Yellow No. 5. Red No. 2 and Violet No. 1 were banned by the FDA in the mid-seventies as possible carcinogens but prior to that were widely used in pet foods.

Interestingly enough, the food colorings are not for the cats. Cats don't care what color the food is. Food colorings are used to satisfy the cat's owner, you, the consumer.

THERE'S MORE!

Sugar is not an ingredient that most people would expect to find in cat food, but many cat foods do contain sugar, especially the semimoist foods. In fact, some semimoist foods contain as much as 15 percent sugar. The sugar adds palatability and moisture, and aids in bacterial contamination prevention. Cats do not need this amount of sugar, which can stress the pancreas and adrenal glands, causing diabetes. Completely devoid of protein, vitamins and minerals, sugar is, literally, empty calories.

Salt is added to many foods as a meat preservative. Too much salt can irritate the digestive system and can cause a mineral imbalance. Salt itself can upset the calcium/potassium balance.

REMEMBER QUALITY

The presence of some or all of the above-listed ingredients, which are the most commonly used cat food ingredients, or an assortment of these ingredients, doesn't necessarily mean that your cat is going to be well nourished. The ingredients must be in the right combinations and of good quality, both before and after processing.

BIOLOGICAL VALUE. The biological values of the ingredients are a key to good nutrition. The biological value of a food is the measurement of the amino acid completeness of the proteins contained by the food. Eggs are considered a wonderful source of protein because they contain all of the essential amino acids. Therefore, eggs have a biological value of 100 percent. Fish meal is 92 percent; beef is 78 percent, as is milk; wheat is 60 percent; wheat gluten is 40; corn is 54 percent. Neither wheat nor corn would be an adequate diet alone, but fed together with one or two meat-based proteins capable of supplying the missing amino acids, they could supply an adequate diet.

For example, Hill's Science Diet Feline Maintenance Light lists as its primary ingredients rice, poultry meal, corn gluten meal and chicken liver. These are varied protein sources, both meat and cereal based, and together make the biological value of the food good.

DIGESTIBILITY. Digestibility refers to the quantity of the food that is actually absorbed by the cat's system. The more food that is fully metabolized, the higher the digestibility figure. During feeding trials, the cats' feces are collected and analyzed to determine the undigested residues of the food eaten. Dr. Steve Hannah, a nutrition scientist with Purina, said, "Digestibility is determined by the amount of food consumed, minus the amount of undigested or unabsorbed food in the stool." High digestibility indicates that the nutrients within a given food are available to be used by the cat.

QUALITY BEFORE PROCESSING. Understanding the definition of an ingredient is not enough. A short description doesn't tell us exactly how good that ingredient is. Many grains grown in poor soil will lack needed vitamins and minerals; unfortunately, this is a common occurrence in the United States. Grains and vegetables can be polluted with fertilizer residues and pesticides of various kinds.

Ingredients can be soiled with mold, mildew and fungus. The quality of meat can be suspect, too. We all have stories of finding bits of hair and other unsavory additives in our hamburger—the quality of meats used for cat foods is much lower. The U.S. Department of Agriculture (USDA) has said that there is no mandatory federal inspection of ingredients used in pet food manufacturing. However, some states do inspect manufacturing plants, especially those producing canned foods.

In the majority of states it is legal (and common practice) for pet food manufacturers to use what are known as "4-D" meat sources: animals that are dead, dying, diseased or disabled when they arrive at the slaughterhouse. Dr. P. F. McGargle, a veterinarian and a former federal meat inspector, believes that feeding slaughterhouse wastes to pet animals increases their chances of getting cancer and other degenerative diseases. He said, "Those wastes include moldy, rancid or spoiled processed meats, as well as tissues too severely riddled with cancer to be eaten by people."

Richard H. Pitcairn, DVM, PhD, and Susan Hubble Pitcairn, authors of *Dr. Pitcairn's Complete Guide to Natural Health for Dogs and Cats* (Rodale Books, 1982), remind us of another group of additives that has been left off the cat food labels: hormones, insecticides and other chemicals. The majority of livestock used for food production are loaded with growth hormones, pesticides, antibiotics and other chemicals. Meat from fetal tissues of pregnant cows is naturally high in hormones, and high cooking temperatures do not get rid of them.

Dr. Steve Kritsick, a veterinarian specializing in nutrition, said in his *AKC Gazette* column, "Nutrition and Health: You Get What You Pay For" (November 1985) that although the biggest difference between price brand (supermarket), generic and major brand pet foods to most consumers is price, it is not the most important difference. "The adage 'You get what you pay for' is all too true with pet food. Because consumers cannot look at the label and know whether or not a product is safe, animal lovers should consider the reputation of the manufacturer and the recommendation of their veterinarian."

WHAT DO THE CAT FOOD COMPANIES SAY?

While researching this book, and its companion book, *The Consumer's Guide to Dog Food*, I called several major dog and cat food manufacturers, including the makers of most of the top-sellers, to ask them about this issue. In each instance, I was not able to immediately speak to someone other than a receptionist, so I left a message. The same message was left with all of the companies contacted. I started with my name and telephone number, an introduction, and what my research was for. The questions I asked were:

1. Many experts seem to feel that there are many instances of poor quality or tainted ingredients being used in dog and cat foods. How is a consumer to know what the quality of the food is? Is price the only way to tell? Does the consumer really get what he or she pays for?

2. What are the differences between the food you are manufacturing and other foods on the market, in regards to the quality of ingredients?
3. Where do the ingredients for your foods come from and what quality control is used for those ingredients?

Guess what? No one answered my questions. No one at all. Now, when I formulated the questions, I realized they were quite pointed, and might be uncomfortable with some of the companies. However, by leaving a message and allowing the companies time to formulate an answer, I was sure that I would at least get a response.

I may be off-base, but to me, as a consumer who buys quite a bit of dog and cat food each month, the total lack of response bothered me. I understand that perhaps the spokesperson didn't know the answers. Or if the companies buy in bulk from grain brokers, perhaps there is no way to know what some of the answers are; in that case, an "I don't know" would have been appropriate. Unfortunately, the total lack of response said to me that the companies I contacted didn't want to answer the questions at all.

QUALITY AFTER PROCESSING. Many nutrients—especially enzymes and some vitamins and minerals—can be damaged by the high temperatures used in processing pet foods. If the nutrients are in the raw food but are damaged in processing, obviously they are not going to help your cat.

NUTRITIONAL ADEQUACY CLAIM

Some experts take issue with the claim that some dog and cat food manufacturers make that their food is "100 percent complete for all life stages." In John Cargill's article, "Feed that Dog! Part III" (*Dog World* magazine, September 1993), Dr. Randy Wysong said, "Thus, that which is absurd in human nutrition has become commonplace, expected and even mandated in pet nutrition." He continued by saying that the "100 percent complete" concept ignores the fact that each dog and cat is an individual, with individual needs. He also said, "We don't have complete knowledge of what nutrition a pet requires." He went on to discuss other unknowns, including what damage processing causes to ingredients and what the dog or cat actually digests from its food.

MANUFACTURERS' ADDRESSES
& PHONE NUMBERS

This is provided so that if you have any questions or problems with the product, you can ask about them.

IN CLOSING

Cat food labels do provide quite a bit of information; learning how to decipher them can take some time. However, the time to do that is not when you are standing in the aisle looking at the rows of foods available. Instead, study the foods at home. Most cat food manufacturers provide pet stores and veterinarians with samples; these are yours for the asking. If you get a variety of samples, you can study the labels at home, at your leisure.

As you study them, keep in mind that there is also much information not freely given on the label, such as the quality of the ingredients used. As we know, this information can be difficult to come by and you may need to rely upon the recommendation of experts, including your veterinarian, the philosophy and reputation of the company and the price of the food itself.

CHART 13
DRY MATTER BASIS CONVERSION

The labels of dry, canned, frozen or semimoist foods look very much alike until you get to the guaranteed analysis, which looks different. The dry food will probably have a protein percentage of between 26 and 32, while canned foods have protein percentages of about 8 to 12. Why are they so different? Primarily because of the moisture content, which will be about 65 to 80 percent for canned food and 3 to 10 percent in dry.

To compare the foods and get a good idea of what the foods really are, you must remove the moisture from the guaranteed analysis and compare both foods as dry matter.

For Dry Food

Brand X dry food:	Guaranteed Analysis
Protein	20%
Fat	10%
Fiber	10%
Moisture	10%

If a dry food shows that the moisture level is 10 percent, that means the dry solid matter in the food is 90 percent. To find the protein level of this dry matter, divide the 20 percent protein (from the label) by 90 percent dry solids. The answer, 22 percent, is the percentage of protein in the actual dry food.

For Canned Food

Brand Z canned food:	Guaranteed Analysis
Protein	5%
Fat	5%
Fiber	10%
Moisture	80%

The conversion for canned food is the same. If the moisture level is 80 percent, that means the dry solids in this food is 20 percent. To find the protein levels of this food, the 5 percent protein (from the label) is divided by the 20 percent dry solids. The answer, 25 percent, is the protein level of the dry solid matter food.

The fat levels of a particular food can be figured using the same formula, substituting the fat percentage from the label. And so on.

CHART 14
FIRST FIVE INGREDIENTS:
POPULAR DRY FOODS

Alpo Seafood Flavor
1. ground yellow corn
2. poultry by-products meal
3. corn gluten meal
4. fish meal
5. soybean meal

Century Pet Care Carnivore
1. chicken by-products meal
2. brewer's rice
3. whole ground corn
4. chicken fat
5. corn gluten meal

Friskies Kitten
1. ground yellow corn
2. poultry by-products meal
3. digest—chicken by-products, fish, fish by-products
4. corn gluten meal
5. soybean meal

Hills' Science Diet Growth
1. poultry by-products meal
2. ground corn
3. animal fat
4. corn gluten meal
5. dried whole egg

CHART 14, CONTINUED

Iams Lamb and Rice
1. lamb
2. rice flour
3. chicken by-products meal
4. ground corn
5. animal fat

Natura Innova
1. turkey
2. chicken meal
3. chicken
4. potatoes
5. eggs

Nutro Max Kitten
1. chicken meal
2. corn gluten meal
3. wheat flour
4. ground rice
5. poultry fat

Old Mother Hubbard Neura
1. brewer's rice
2. poultry by-products meal
3. corn gluten meal
4. animal fat
5. dried whole egg

Purina Cat Chow
1. ground corn
2. corn gluten meal
3. soybean meal
4. poultry by-products meal
5. animal fat

Purina Cat Chow Special Care
1. corn gluten meal
2. ground corn
3. chicken
4. beef tallow
5. brewer's rice

Purina ONE
1. corn gluten meal
2. ground corn
3. chicken
4. brewer's rice
5. wheat flour

Sensible Choice Kitten Chicken and Rice
1. chicken meal
2. brewer's rice
3. rice flour
4. chicken
5. chicken fat

Sensible Choice Chicken and Rice
1. chicken meal
2. brewer's rice
3. rice flour
4. chicken
5. chicken fat

Wal-Mart Special Kitty
1. ground yellow corn
2. poultry by-products meal
3. ground wheat
4. corn gluten meal
5. soybean meal

CHART 15
FIRST FIVE INGREDIENTS:
POPULAR CANNED FOODS

Alpo Grill
1. meat by-products
2. fish
3. water
4. poultry by-products
5. beef

Friskies Kitten Ocean Whitefish
1. Ocean whitefish
2. Meat by-products
3. fish
4. water
5. nonfat milk

Friskies Kitten Mixed Grill
1. meat by-products
2. beef
3. water
4. fish
5. poultry

Heinz 9 Lives Plus Turkey and Rice
1. water
2. turkey
3. meat by-products
4. poultry by-products
5. liver

Hill's Science Diet Growth
1. water
2. liver
3. chicken
4. whole egg
5. poultry by-products

Hill's Science Diet Maintenance Lite

1. water
2. meat by-products
3. liver
4. ground corn
5. powdered cellulose

Iams Less Active Fish and Rice

1. water
2. whitefish
3. beef
4. beef liver
5. beef by-products

Iams Less Active Chicken and Rice

1. water
2. chicken
3. chicken liver
4. beef by-products
5. whitefish

Iams Beef

1. beef liver
2. water
3. beef
4. egg
5. chicken fat

Kal Kan Optimum Seafood

1. water
2. poultry by-products
3. oceanfish
4. meat by-products
5. meat by-products

Nature's Recipe Optimum Chicken

1. chicken stock
2. chicken
3. chicken by-products
4. chicken liver
5. rice

CHART 15, CONTINUED

Nutro Max Lite
1. chicken
2. chicken broth
3. defatted rice bran
4. brewer's rice
5. lamb liver

Purina Rainbow Trout
1. water
2. chicken
3. rainbow trout
4. liver
5. whitefish

Waltham Senior Diet Chicken
1. water
2. chicken
3. chicken by-products
4. meat by-products
5. liver

Waltham Lite Chicken
1. water
2. chicken
3. chicken by-products
4. beef by-products
5. meat by-products

Waltham Growth Chicken
1. meat by-products
2. water
3. chicken
4. chicken liver and heart
5. beef by-products

CHART 16
DRY FOOD PRESERVATIVES AS
LISTED ON THE LABEL

Company	Food	Preservatives Used
Alpo Cat Food	Seafood	BHA, citric acid
Century Pet Care	Carnivore	tocopherols
Friskies	Kitten	BHA, ethoxyquin
Hill's Science Diet	Growth	BHA, ethoxyquin
Hill's Science Diet	Maintenance	BHA, ethoxyquin, citric acid
Iams	Lamb and Rice	tocopherols
Iams	Less Active	BHA, ethoxyquin
Iams	Cat Food	BHA, ethoxyquin
Natura	Innova	Vitamins E and C
Nutro Max	Kitten	ethoxyquin
Nutro Max	Lite	ethoxyquin
Old Mother Hubbard	Neura	Vitamin E, citric acid
Purina	Cat Chow Special Care	tocopherols
Purina	Cat Chow	BHA
Purina	Kit 'N Kaboodle	BHA
Purina	ONE	tocopherols
Sensible Choice	Chicken and Rice	tocopherols
Sensible Choice	Kitten	tocopherols
Wal-Mart	Special Kitty	BHA, citric acid

SIX

CHOOSING THE RIGHT FOOD FOR YOUR CAT

There are, literally, thousands of different cat foods available. There are canned foods, dry kibble, semimoist and frozen foods. Some foods are incredibly expensive and others are very cheap. There are very nutritious, complete cat foods made with ingredients approved for human use and other foods of dubious nutritional value with very questionable ingredients. Some foods are nationally advertised while others are known in small geographical areas and promoted by word of mouth.

To make matters even more confusing, there are specialty foods: foods for cats with specific needs. Almost all manufacturers have special foods for kittens, for adults and for older cats. There are also diet foods for overweight cats, special foods for pregnant or lactating queens, high calorie foods for active, showing or stressed cats and special foods for cats with health problems.

How can you sift through this cornucopia of foods and narrow the field down to one? Again, knowledge is the key. Knowledge of the foods, what they are and what the terms mean.

Keep in mind, too, that many of the foods available were actually made for the cat's owner. David Mayberry of Iams Pet Foods said, "The varieties of flavors and imitation meats are aimed at the consumer and have no bearing on nutritional values." Cats don't care whether or not their food is shaped like tiny fishes but many owners think they do.

CLASSIFICATIONS OF FOODS

There are three basic classifications of cat foods: economy, regular and premium. Cat foods have been rated or placed into classifications because all cat foods are not created equal (although most manufacturers and their advertising firms would like to have you think so). The types of classifications are not as important as is why they exist and where the different foods fit. Let's look at them.

ECONOMY BRANDS

Cat foods that are listed in the economy classifications are usually the generic brand cat foods. These foods are usually available at grocery stores, feed stores or at discount department stores. Economy foods are very inexpensive and are made of the cheapest ingredients available. As a result, they usually consist of poorer grade ingredients. Their energy values are usually lower, as are their protein sources and digestibility.

The Veterinary Medical Teaching Hospital at the University of California at Davis has identified what is being called "generic dog food associated disease." This is essentially nutritional deficiencies that appear in dogs who have been fed economy-type dog foods. The disease or syndrome may show up as slow or retarded growth, skeletal abnormalities, poor hair coat, skin disorders, even behavior problems. Similar studies are now being conducted with cats although the results are not yet available.

REGULAR BRANDS

Regular or mid-range cat foods are in the middle between economy and premium cat foods. These foods cost less than premium foods but more than economy. They have better quality ingredients from better sources. These foods are often found at grocery stores, feed stores and some pet shops.

PREMIUM BRANDS

Premium foods use better quality ingredients from better food sources with higher biological values. Consequently, their digestibility is higher. Whereas an economy or regular brand of cat food might use corn, wheat or soybean as the primary ingredient, a premium-quality food will be more likely to use a good quality meat source as the main ingredient.

Because premium foods are made of better quality ingredients and have a better digestibility, the cat needs to eat much less food than he would need to consume of a lesser quality food. Premium foods have another advantage that is important to many cat owners and that is the fact that there is less waste in premium foods. (Less waste translates as less fecal matter to scoop out of the litter box.)

FORMS OF FOODS AND THEIR PROS AND CONS
Most cat foods come in one of four different forms:

1. dry
2. canned
3. semimoist
4. frozen

DRY FOOD. The most popular form of cat food is dry food. Dry cat food usually has a moisture content of 10 to 12 percent or less and contains meats and meat products, grains, vegetables and other ingredients. Most dry foods are made using an extruder, a machine that can cook the food at a high temperature for a very short period of time. Dry cat foods are usually sold in bagged form, from 4 to 40 or 50 pounds per bag or in smaller boxes weighing about 18 ounces. The shelf life is normally three to six months, depending upon the method of preservation used.

Pros: Dry cat foods have a good shelf life, are easy to serve and store and are the most reasonable in price. There is little annoying odor, and the scraping motion that takes place as the cat eats can assist in the cat's dental care. Most cats will readily accept dry food.

Cons: The only drawback to dry food is that cats used to eating canned or semimoist foods will sometimes resist a change to dry food. For this reason, some owners "spice" up the dry food by adding a little canned food to it.

CANNED FOODS. Higher quality canned cat foods are primarily meat products with a high moisture content, usually about 70 to 80 percent. Canned foods can and do contain other ingredients than meat, some of which can be visibly seen in the food, other, which are combined with other ingredients and are not as noticeable, like corn meal.

Pros: Canned foods are very palatable to the cat, especially the foods made primarily of meat. Canned foods also have a very long shelf life.

Cons: Canned foods do not help scrape tartar off the cat's teeth. Canned foods can have an objectionable odor (to the cat's owner, anyway, although the cats seem to like it!). Canned foods are more expensive than dry foods.

FROZEN FOODS. Frozen cat foods (packaged in a loaf form) are very high in meat ingredients and in moisture content, about 60 to 70 percent. These food can also contain other ingredients than meat, depending upon the food. The shelf life of these foods varies, depending upon the processing and the ingredients. The date is usually on the package. Cost also varies, depending upon the ingredients and the brand.

Pros: When thawed, frozen foods are very palatable and most cats eagerly eat the food. Unused portions should remain in the freezer, making it less likely to spoil.

Cons: Because the food is served thawed and soft, it does nothing to assist in your cat's dental care. Because it must be thawed ahead of time, more thought and planning is required on your part to feed the cat.

SEMIMOIST FOODS. Semimoist foods are somewhere in between canned and dry foods in moisture content. Most have a moisture content of about 30 percent. Many of these foods list meat as one of the first five ingredients, but they also contain a variety of other ingredients, including sugar or sugar products.

Pros: These foods are usually packaged in individual servings, making them easy to store and use.

Cons: As was previously mentioned, semimoist foods often contain great amounts of sugar, not a good source of nutrition for cats. Semimoist foods are also more expensive than dry foods, do not help with dental care and usually contain a number of artificial colors, flavorings and preservatives.

MIXING FOODS

Many cat owners mix dry and canned foods on a regular basis. Some owners feel that dry food is unappetizing or boring. Some cats have convinced their owners that they will not eat plain dry food. Whatever the reason owners choose to mix dry and canned foods, some experts feel that a mixture might be the better answer anyway.

Mike Guerber, a manager for Precise Pet Products, said, "Canned food is a very important part of feline nutrition." A study showed that the enzymes produced when cats ate both dry and canned foods resulted in better digestion and utilization of both foods.

Guerber emphasized, though, that the foods should both be of high quality. "If you want to give your cat a premium dry food because of its superior nutrition, why would you want to dilute that with an inferior canned food?" A ratio of 75 to 80 percent dry food and 20 to 25 percent canned food seems to be an accepted balance with most experts.

COST OF CAT FOODS

When comparing like forms of cat foods—different brands of canned foods to each other, or dry foods to other dry foods—cost does often indicate quality. Because the ingredients needed for premium cat foods are of better quality, they cost more. At the same time, processing is, in most cases, also of better quality for premium foods. All of these costs are passed on to you, the consumer. Therefore, the premium cat foods do cost more.

In the long run, though, they are worth what you pay for them. Most cats require less food when eating a premium brand food because the food is more digestible. The health benefits alone make a premium food a better bargain. Fewer stools in the litter box are an additional incentive.

FOODS FOR ALL AGES AND BREEDS

KITTEN FORMULAS. Growth (kitten) foods are made by most of the larger cat food manufacturers. A kitten food should supply enough nutrition for growth, play and good health. Most of these foods are made with higher protein levels than adult formulas, generally in dry food the protein is between 30 to 35 percent. Fat levels are also higher, usually from 15 to 20 percent, than in dry food.

Most kitten foods also contain supplements of vitamins and minerals. However, keep in mind that more of these substances is not always better. As was mentioned in Chapter Four, oversupplementation of vitamins A, D, K and E can cause toxicity. An imbalance of calcium and phosphorus can have disastrous results. Therefore, read the label, look for a balance in the food and don't hesitate to call the manufacturer if you have questions.

ADULT FORMULAS. Maintenance or adult foods should meet the needs of the majority of adult cats. This food is for the so-called "average" cat, if there is really such a thing. An adult formula should supply enough calories for day to day living, exercise and good health.

The protein levels in most premium dry adult maintenance foods is usually 28 and 32 percent with fat levels between 10 and 20 percent. Again, vitamin and mineral supplementation is important, but if you have questions, call the manufacturer.

REDUCED CALORIE FORMULAS. Some experts have said that obesity is America's number one health problem. Unfortunately, the same goes for America's cats; more cats are overweight today than ever before, and it can have some lasting effects on these cats' health.

In response, a number of manufacturers are offering reduced calorie cat foods. Most of these foods offer reduced protein and fat levels and higher fiber. Protein averages between 28 to 32 percent for most of the foods, with fat anywhere from 8 to 10 percent. The higher fiber levels (8 to 10 percent) serve a number of purposes including keeping the bowels functioning well. The fiber also helps make the cat feel full, a benefit on any diet.

The challenge of any reduced calorie food is to provide adequate (or better!) nutrition while allowing the cat to feel full and cutting calories at the same time. A greatly reduced protein and fat percentage could hamper the cat's ability to thrive, remain active and healthy. Therefore, many veterinarians recommend feeding a premium food with at least 30 percent protein, 8 to 10 percent fat and then increasing the cat's daily exercise.

SENIOR/GERIATRIC FORMULAS. A debate is ongoing as to whether older cats should have reduced amounts of protein or not. One side of the argument states that senior cats should have less protein as they age so that the kidneys and liver have to process less protein. The other camp argues that proteins are needed for energy, for tissue repair and for good health. Daniel Carey, DVM, Iams Pet Foods' director of technical communications, said, "A 1994 university study of protein and older dogs and cats showed no adverse effects of protein on kidney function."

However, once a cat has kidney disease, most experts do agree that a lower protein food is usually advised. Also, as cats age, their metabolism usually slows down and, as a result, many older cats can gain weight, even when they are eating a food that has served them well all along. In these cases, reduced calories are a good idea.

If you have doubt as to whether or not your cat should eat a senior or geriatric food, call the cat food manufacturers of the foods you are examining, tell them about your cat and ask them about their food. Also, talk to your veterinarian and get his or her input.

PRESCRIPTION DIETS. These diet formulas are called prescription or therapeutic diets because they are sold through veterinarians. These diets are formulated as a nutritional aid for specific health problems, including heart disease, renal failure, pancreatitis, diabetes, gastrointestinal disorders, skin disease and more.

Several companies make prescription diets. Hill's Pet Nutrition, makers of Science Diet foods, makes a line called Prescription Diet. Pro Plan makes Clinical Nutrition Management and Vet's Choice makes Select Care nutritional aids.

The decision to change your cat to one of these diets should be made with your veterinarian. Not only is the food sold through your veterinarian but some of these diets are quite different and your vet should monitor your cat as you change its food.

CHART 17
ECONOMY—PREMIUM FOOD COMPARISON

Economy Food	Premium Food
Lower purchase price	Higher purchase price
Primary Ingredient: corn, wheat, soybeans	Primary Ingredient: good quality meat product
Low biological value	Higher biological value
Poor digestibility	Higher digestibility
Large feces	Smaller, firm stools
Low energy value	Higher energy value
Often makes claims: "For all life stages" "Meaty flavor" "Looks like..."	Claims are easily proven Ingredients don't change
Ingredients can change depending upon market availability	

CHART 18
ASSESSING YOUR CAT'S NUTRITIONAL NEEDS: A WORKSHEET

Note: The purpose of this questionnaire is to help you decide upon the cat foods that meet or satisfy your needs as a responsible cat owner as well as your cat's individual nutritional needs. By answering the questions as honestly as possible (no one will see it but you!) you can then analyze the foods available and choose the best food for you both.

YOUR NEEDS:

Do you have any particular concerns about the quality of cat food ingredients? _____

Are there any preservatives, chemicals or artificial colors you would rather your cat not eat? _____

Are there any food ingredients you would like to avoid? _____
_____

Are there any ingredients you would like your cat to eat? _____
_____

CHART 18, CONTINUED

Is cost of the cat food a factor? _____

If price is important, what are you willing to spend? _____

Analysis: Make sure you understand how to read the labels on the cat food packages so that you can chose a food of high quality with good ingredients and so that you can include or exclude particular ingredients. Call the manufacturer if you have questions about particular ingredients, preservatives or additives. Keep in mind that it may not be possible to combine your philosophical beliefs with your cat's nutritional needs.

YOUR CAT'S HEALTH:

Is your cat of a breed that has known genetic disorders that affect or can be affected by food? _____

Is your cat a member of a breed with specific, known nutritional needs?

_____

Has your cat been seen by its veterinarian within the last six months?

_____

What is your cat's state of health today? _____

Does the cat have any ongoing health problems? _____

Could any of these be diet related? _____

Could a special diet help ease any of these problems? _____

Does your cat have any confirmed or suspected food allergies? _____
     If yes, what are they?_____

Is your cat going to be bred? _____

Analysis: Make sure you have a good working relationship with your cat's veterinarian and talk to him or her about your cat's nutritional needs. As we have learned in previous chapters, diet can have significant effects on a cat's health.

We know, too, that specific breeds sometimes have different requirements. If your breeder and veterinarian cannot help you with information about your breed, you may wish to contact the national breed club. (Addresses can often be found in the national magazines devoted to cats, such as *Cat Fancy* or *Cats* magazines.) Also, a pregnant or lactating queen has specific needs from her food.

YOUR CAT'S AGE:

How old is your cat? _____

Could your cat benefit from an age-related specialty food, such as kitten food or senior food? _____

Analysis: There are many age specific foods available and these formulations are certainly something to consider when choosing a food. However, age is not the only factor; instead, it is simply one piece of your cat's nutritional puzzle. Many, many kittens have grown up and thrived on adult cat foods and many older cats have never eaten a bite of a senior food.

YOUR CAT'S ACTIVITY LEVEL:

How much exercise does your cat get on a daily basis? _____

Does your cat participate in cat shows? _____

Does your cat have a lean body type combined with a constantly busy personality? _____

Analysis: Many cats can maintain an active life while eating a premium brand, adult maintenance formula food. However, a very active or stressed cat might need some supplementation.

YOUR CAT'S EMOTIONAL HEALTH:

Does your cat have any behavior problems? _____

Does your cat enjoy its play sessions? _____

How does your cat handle stress? _____

How does your cat handle changes in its environment? Visitors or guests? Holidays? Changes in the daily routine?

_____

Is your cat often irritable? Depressed? Aggressive? Or unpredictable?

_____

Is your cat mentally alert, bright-eyed and happy? _____

CHART 18, CONTINUED

Analysis: Food allergies can cause a number of different problems, ranging from scratching and red skin to emotional and behavior problems and excessive mood swings. Ask your veterinarian for a referral to an allergist.

Cats without food allergies can also show behavioral problems or signs of stress that can be helped with a high quality diet and herbal supplements.

CHART 19
TASTE TESTS

I conducted these tests for my own information, wanting to check the appeal and palatability of some of the foods. After all, the food is useless unless the cat will eat it. However, these tests are unscientific, conducted only with my personal cats.

To conduct each test, I placed the cat involved in another room while I spread out the food samples, placing the foods a few inches apart on the floor, in a semicircle so that each food would be an equal distance from the cat. I then brought the cat in and set him or her down in the pre-arranged spot. I then watched the cat's reactions. It was interesting to see what the cats chose.

Dry Adult Foods

Test Cat: Squirt, a five-year-old Domestic Shorthair who is a good eater but somewhat picky.

    Foods offered:
        Hill's Science Diet Maintenance
        Purina Cat Show
        Purina Kit 'N Kaboodle
        Alpo Seafood Flavor
        Breeder's Choice APD Feline Formula
        Carnivore

Results: Squirt took a quick bite of the Science Diet maintenance, then promptly moved to the Carnivore and ate the entire sample.

Dry Kitten or Growth Foods

Test Cat: Havoc, a two-year-old British Shorthair. Havoc likes food and is not hesitant about trying new things.

Foods Offered:

Hill's Science Diet Growth
Select Care Development Formula
Sensible Choice Kitten
Friskies Kitten
Purina Kitten Chow Dairy

Results: Havoc nibbled all the samples, tasting each one, but finally finished off the Science Diet Growth.

Canned Adult Foods

Test Cat: Tigger, a fourteen-year-old Domestic Shorthair. Tigger is a good eater, not finicky at all, but also not aggressive about food.

Foods offered:

Sensible Choice Chicken and Rice
Nature's Recipe Optimum Chicken
Nutro Natural Choice Chicken, Lamb and Rice
Waltham Sheba Beef
Kal Kan Optimum Beef
Fancy Feast Beef and Chicken

Results: Tigger looked at this display of foods, sniffed here and there, and then promptly devoured the entire serving of Fancy Feast.

Canned Reducing, Less Active or Special Diets

Test Cat: Troubles is a nine-year-old Domestic Shorthair who has had an ongoing weight problem. She is very familiar with diet formula foods.

Foods offered:

Hill's Prescription Diet C/D
Vet's Choice Select Balance Less Active
Waltham Lite Chicken
Waltham Senior Diet Chicken
Friskies Senior Savory Beef
Friskies Special Diet Turkey

Results: Troubles isn't used to so much food and it showed. She nibbled here and nibbled there. She tried all of the samples but kept going back to the Friskies Senior Savory Beef.

CHART 20
TASTE TEST: THE SPLASH ABOUT FISH!

Many cat owners are convinced that their cat would prefer to eat only foods made from fish and as a result, some cats are fed a diet consisting primarily of tuna. Many cats fed tuna on a regular basis become finicky eaters, eating only tuna or foods containing tuna. Because of it's strong odor, cats learn to focus on the tuna, excluding other foods. In fact, tuna can be so "addicting" that many manufacturers of canned cat foods add tuna to many of their foods so that cats are attracted to it.

Veterinarians even have a phrase to describe these cats, calling them "tuna junkies." This can be a problem because the oil that the tuna is packed in can cause vitamin depletions, leading to serious health disorders. Fish also contains high amounts of minerals which are necessary for good health but which can cause problems for cats with FUS or other urological diseases.

Looking at the broad picture of your cat's nutritional health, fish is good food when fed as part of a balanced, well-rounded diet. However, if your cat is prone to FUS, then less fish should be fed.

Canned Cat Foods Featuring Fish

Test Cat: Havoc, a two-year-old British Shorthair.
    Foods Offered:
        Friskies Fancy Feast Oceanfish
        Friskies Special Diet Ocean Whitefish
        Kal Kan Optimum Seafood Supper with Tuna
        Avo-Cat Ocean Fish
        Alpo Tuna Treat
        Aristocrat Whitefish and Tuna
        Purina Rainbow Trout
        Purina Ocean Whitefish
    Results: Havoc sniffed and sniffed, tasted the Alpo Tuna Treat first, moved on to Kal Kan Seafood Supper with Tuna and finished by eating all of the Fancy Feast Oceanfish.

SEVEN

FEEDING YOUR CAT

This may seem like the simplest and most obvious part of providing for your cat's eating needs, but it, too, can be confusing. There are choices to be made about:

- when to feed your cat
- how to feed your cat
- where to feed
- how much to feed
- how often to feed
- how to evaluate the food
- what to do when you wish to change foods

All of these things contribute to your cat's health.

Keep in mind, you should feed your cat yourself, fixing its food and putting the food in front of it. If you have more than one cat, each cat should have its own bowl, and don't let them switch. When each cat eats from its own bowl, you know who ate what and how much (or how little), who ate quickly (or slowly), who left food in the bowl and who didn't eat at all. After all, a change in eating habits is one of the first signs of illness.

HOW AND WHEN TO FEED?

Some cat owners use the small size paper plates to feed their cat. This can then be thrown away with any leftover food. Other cat owners invest in nice, personalized ceramic bowls. What you use depends upon your tastes, budget and, of course, your cat's preference.

Some cats will eat out of anything, others prefer flat plates. Some cats get acne when they eat from plastic bowls, others hate the sound of their identification tag banging against a metal bowl. Watch your cat, try different things and see what works best.

Kittens should eat three (or even four) times a day until they are about six months old. These meals should be about six hours apart, if possible. Whatever times you choose, be consistent, kittens need a regular routine.

Adult cats can be fed around their owner's schedules, usually once in the morning and once in the evening. Don't feed too close to bedtime, and don't feed immediately before or after vigorous exercise. Like kittens, adult cats thrive on a routine, so stick to regular mealtimes as much as possible.

Don't just put food out and leave it out all day. When left out, food will spoil, go rancid and will attract ants and other insects. Cats that nibble all day long are also the ones who have a tendency to gain weight. Overweight cats in particular should eat a measured amount of food at set times. If you have more than one cat, it's even more important to feed at set times, giving each cat its own bowl, so that you know who ate what and who didn't.

When your cat has finished its food, or walks away from its bowl, pick up the bowl and discard the leftover food. Cats are not scavengers by nature and will rarely touch leftover food. Besides, bacteria proliferates in old food; throw it away.

WHERE TO FEED?

Your kitten or cat should have a quiet place to eat where he will not be disturbed by the family children or dogs. Clean, fresh food and water bowls should be placed in the same place every day. Choose a corner of the kitchen, a pantry or a hallway where the cat can enjoy his meal relatively uninterrupted. An area where people are constantly coming and going is not a good spot; all the activity will distract the cat from the meal and may cause him to either gulp the meal or to ignore it completely. You can feed more than one cat in the same area as long as their individual bowls are far enough apart so they don't need to be territorial about it. Watch so that the cat who eats faster doesn't try to steal the other cat's food.

HOW MUCH TO FEED?

The label on the cat food will list suggested feeding amounts. For example, the label on Friskies Kitten dry food says that a kitten between four and eight weeks of age should be offered one-third a cup of dry food per day; a kitten between eight weeks and five months should be offered three-quarters of a cup per day; and a kitten between six and twelve months should eat one cup daily.

For most cats, this is just a suggested starting point. In fact, the manufacturers' suggested feeding amounts are sometimes way off what an individual cat really needs. So how do you know how much to feed your cat? Ask yourself these questions:

- How active is your cat? Activity level definitely affects how much food the animal needs. A very active cat will need more calories than a cat that spends all day sleeping.
- What kind of climate do you live in? Weather also affects how much food a cat will need. If your cat goes outside in the cold, he will need more calories to keep warm. But even inside cats will need more calories in the winter in a cold climate.
- How many treats or scraps does your cat get during the day? And be honest with yourself! If your cat gets treats during the day, he will need less food at mealtime. Think of treats as part of your cat's daily food intake. Don't let too many treats spoil the nutritional balance of your cat's food.

HOW OFTEN TO FEED?

Kittens should eat three to four times a day with the largest meal in the morning. If the meals can be spread out equally during the day, that is best. Even though it seems to be traditional to feed adult cats once a day, most do better on two meals, with the largest meal in the morning. Cats fed once a day have a tendency to beg—because they are hungry—and often get irritable because of hunger or low blood sugar.

EVALUATING THE RESULTS

After your cat has been eating a food for four to six weeks, you can evaluate the results to see if the results are what you want.

- Does your cat's coat look healthy? Does it shine? Or is it dull and brittle?
- Is your cat's skin smooth and pliant? Or is it dry and scaly? Is it blotchy or itchy?
- Are your cat's eyes bright and alert?
- Is your cat at a good weight, neither too fat nor too thin? (For a good weight, you should be able to feel ribs under the skin without them actually showing through the skin.)

- Is your cat eating all of its food?
- Is your cat's activity level normal or better than it used to be? Does your cat want to chase a toy, pounce and play?
- Are your cat's stools firm, dark (but not black) and have relatively little odor?

If your cat is eating well, leaving little food, and has a good activity level, and if your cat's skin, coat and eyes appear clean, clear and blemish-free, he should be getting the nutrition he needs from his food. If there is a problem with any of the answers, you may wish to look again at the food your cat is eating. If you have any doubts, talk to your veterinarian as there may be an underlying health problem.

CHANGING YOUR CAT'S FOOD

If you decide to change the food you are feeding your cat, don't do so abruptly. Some cats will refuse to eat when their food is changed and others will suffer severe gastrointestinal upset, complete with diarrhea and vomiting. Changes in the cat's diets must be made gradually.

Start making the change prior to running out of the cat's old food. When you have about three weeks of food left, buy some of the new food. For the first week of the change, feed three-quarters old food and one-quarter new food. Add a little of the new food to the old food, increasing the amount of new food each week. By the fourth week, you can feed the new food entirely.

CHANGING YOUR CAT'S FOOD

Ideally, changing brands of food or other components of your cat's diet should take place over a period of three weeks. The first week, feed your cat one-quarter (25%) of the new food and three-quarters (75%) of its old food. The second week, feed your cat 50/50: half the old food and half the new food. During the third week, feed three-quarters (75%) the new food and one quarter (25%) the old food. By the fourth week, the cat should be eating the new food with little or no gastrointestinal upset.

EIGHT

SUPPLEMENTS: SHOULD YOU OR SHOULDN'T YOU?

Most nutritionists and veterinarians consider a supplement to be anything that is added to the cat's diet on a regular basis. Therefore, if you add some yogurt to your cat's food each day, that is a supplement. If you add a multivitamin/mineral tablet, that, too, is a supplement. There are a number of other supplements that are commonly used by cat owners; some commercial preparations, others are homemade.

Should you use supplements? As with so many aspects of feline nutrition, the experts' opinions vary. Some, especially those researchers working with pet food manufacturers, say that a good quality food is all a cat needs. However, many other experts say that even a "balanced and complete" cat food is not always enough, that it doesn't take into consideration each cat's individual needs and the actual quality and digestibility of the cat food.

Richard Pitcairn, DVM, states in his book, *Dr. Pitcairn's Complete Guide to Natural Health for Dogs & Cats* (Rodale Books, 1982), "I always recommend the inclusion of several nutrition packed food supplements in the (cat's) diet." He continued by saying that those supplements are recommended because they fortify the diet with plenty of important vitamins and minerals. The diet the cat eats may be lacking in nutrition due to soil depletion as well as storage and cooking procedures. Dr. Pitcairn also believes that the stress and pollution we take for granted as part of modern life can cause nutritional deficiencies.

Dr. Clarence Hardin, the director of the California Mobile Veterinary Service and a known preventative medicine vet, recommends a number of dietary supplements. He says, "Today's pets face a number of critical health dangers, including air and water pollution and substandard, chemically-laden foods. Often traditional nutrition and medicine is not enough."

Other experts recommend supplements for specific situations, such as for cats under stress or those with health problems. Supplements of specific types are also often recommended for cats with health disorders, especially diseases affecting nutrition or digestion.

DECIDING TO SUPPLEMENT

Deciding what supplements to add to the cat's diet is often difficult. Some cat owners see an advertisement for a new product that is supposed to be on the "cutting edge" of nutrition while other cat owners hear or read about a supplement that is supposed to accomplish something specific, such as produce healthy skin, and they start adding that to their cat's diet. Other cat owners do a lot of research, searching out exactly the right nutrients for their cat.

As long as the supplement itself is not harmful to the cat, and the amount given is appropriate to the cat's size, condition and general health, the only real danger with supplementing a diet is that the supplement may unbalance a previous balanced, complete food. However, most experts agree that if commercial supplements are given according to directions and homemade supplements do not total over 10 percent of the food eaten, they are probably safe.

When giving supplements, it is important that the cat's overall condition and health is watched closely. If there appears to be any kind of an allergic reaction, stop the supplement and call your veterinarian. If there is any detrimental change in the cat's condition or health, again, stop the supplement and talk to your veterinarian.

Keep in mind, too, that if you are trying to accomplish something specific with the supplement, such as improve skin and coat condition, food supplements take time to work. It may take a few weeks before you see any change in your cat's skin and even two to three months before you see any change in the cat's coat.

COMMERCIALLY AVAILABLE SUPPLEMENTS

ENZYME FORMULAS. Enzyme formulas are designed to enhance or replace naturally occurring enzymes. Pancreatic enzymes are often recommended as supplements for cats that are no longer producing enough enzymes on their own. Other enzyme supplements are derived from plant sources, such as papain or bromelain.

Enzyme supplements can be especially beneficial when a cat is on a high fiber diet. Fiber is known to interfere with zinc absorption in the intestinal tract and additional enzymes can free up those and other nutrients in the fiber, making them more available for metabolism by the cat.

One popular formula, Prozyme, is advertised as "Enhancing the bioavailability of all pet foods." It is supposed to work directly on the food by replacing the natural enzymes lost due to processing.

FATTY ACID FORMULAS. There are a number of fatty acid supplements available commercially and most are advertised as beneficial to the skin and coat. Most of these are supposed to be high in essential fatty acids, especially linoleic and arachidonic acids. These are usually recommended for cats with skin allergies or other disorders, including dietary deficiencies, that are causing poor hair coat, dry skin or excessive shedding.

VITAMIN/MINERAL SUPPLEMENTS. There are probably as many vitamin/mineral supplements available for cats as there are for people. Cat owners can purchase complete vitamin/mineral preparations or they can buy supplements containing one specific vitamin or mineral.

When supplementing a commercial food, it's important to know what vitamins and minerals the food contains and in what amounts because with many vitamins and minerals, too much is just as dangerous as too little. If you are in doubt as to what your cat is getting from its food, call the manufacturer and ask.

Sometimes individual vitamins or minerals are recommended for a specific purpose. Charts 10 and 12 in Chapter Four discuss vitamin and mineral deficiencies (as well as excesses) and can serve as a guideline as to what you may want to supplement.

Source Plus! Micronutrients is a commercially available product that is derived from dehydrated seaweeds and contains over 60 different vitamins, macrominerals and microminerals (trace minerals). The literature for Source Plus! states, "All 50 states in the United States have reported mineral deficiencies in farmland soils, deficiencies which work their way up the food chain into the diets of horses, dogs, cats and humans."

FOOD SUPPLEMENTS. A few supplements are available that are made from foods rather than simpler food forms, such as vitamins, minerals, fatty acids or enzymes. Most of these supplements are designed to provide more complete nutrition for cats, aiding what might otherwise be a less than complete diet.

#1 All Systems, a company known for its grooming products, has produced a supplement called Vital Energy. Made from flax seed, molasses, yeast, rice bran, liver, alfalfa and a number of other quality ingredients, Vital Energy contains antioxidants, phytochemicals, enzymes, amino acids, trace minerals and vitamins. Vital Energy is itself a balanced food, eliminating the concern of oversupplementation.

HERBAL SUPPLEMENTS

Herbs have been used as nutritional supplements and as preventative and curative medicine for thousands of years. Thanks to antibiotics, aspirin and other "magic bullets," the use of herbs decreased over the last century. However, people have discovered that those magic bullets are not all powerful and the use of herbs has increased significantly over the last decade.

Again, as with many aspects of feline nutrition, the experts— nutritionists, veterinarians and researchers—vary on the use of herbs as supplements. Some are outspoken in their beliefs that herbs are, literally, "old wives' tales." Other experts answer back with the statement that those old wives kept mankind and mankind's domestic animals alive for thousands of years prior to the dawn of modern medicine.

Herbs must be used carefully. Anita Frazier, a noted feline nutritionist and behaviorist and author of *The New Natural Cat* (Plume, 1990), said about herbs, "Some herbs are harmless and some can damage the system if used carelessly. Keep in mind that some herbs work differently on cats than they do on humans. Catnip, for example, is a stimulant and aphrodisiac for a cat while humans take the tea as a sedative." Frazier recommends that all cat owners research thoroughly any herb before giving it to their cat.

The herbs listed below are those whose use is more widely accepted. If you or your veterinarian have any questions as to dosage, side effects or if you simply want more information, check with your local health food store or check the bibliography in the back of this book for more reading.

Alfalfa. Alfalfa (which means the father of all foods) is full of trace minerals, vitamins A, E, K, B and D. It has also been used to alleviate the pain and stiffness of arthritis and the discomfort of stomach ailments.

Burdock root is cooked like a carrot, is high in organic iron and vitamin C and is soothing to the gastrointestinal tract.

Catnip is probably best known herb for cats. Dried, this herb is a stimulant and an aphrodisiac. Used too much, more than twice a week or so, it loses its attraction.

Red clover is a stimulant for healing and is good for a recuperating cat or an older cat.

Dandelions are known to help the body filter toxins from the system.

Echinacea is an herb known by experts to stimulate the immune system, so much so that physicians are even recommending it to their human patients during flu season.

Garlic has antibacterial, antifungal and antiviral properties. Whole books have been written about the wonders of garlic. Garlic boosts the immune system and stimulates the internal organs, especially the liver and colon, helping to rid the body of toxins.

Ginseng is often called a wonder drug. This root is known to strengthen the heart, builds general mental and physical vitality and stimulates the endocrine glands, which control the body's systems. Ginseng is a preventative, which means it is not given as medicine but rather as a daily supplement.

Rose hips are really not herbs in the true definition but are instead the seed pods left after a rose blossom passes by. Rose hips are full of vitamins, including A, B, E, K and more vitamin C than any other food we know; even more than citrus fruits. However, rose hips should only be used when they are free of insecticides, fertilizers and fungicides.

FOOD SUPPLEMENTS

Many foods are known to have special nutritional significance; others are known to have medicinal properties. As with herbs, experts disagree as to exactly how important these foods are. Again, if you want more information, or have any doubts, ask questions at your local health food store, talk to your veterinarian or check the bibliography of this book for more information. Listed below are foods whose properties are more widely known and accepted.

Barley is a grain and has recently been used more frequently in cat foods. Barley is known to improve bowel function and is thought to possibly inhibit cancer.

Broccoli is known to inhibit cancer and is also a great source of many vitamins, including vitamin A.

Carrots are a wonderful source of beta-carotene but they also contain other vitamins as well as many trace minerals.

Cranberry juice is known to have beneficial effects on the urinary tract, preventing infections and cystitis. Cranberry juice is also recognized as having strong antiviral properties.

Fish, especially saltwater fish, have a number of nutritional benefits. Ingestion of as little as one ounce of saltwater fish daily is known to boost the immune system, inhibit cancer, combat kidney disease and increase mental alertness.

Kelp is a type of seaweed. It is usually sold dried and ground to a fine powder, often encased in gel capsules. Kelp is an excellent mineral supplement as it is high in iodine, calcium and potassium as well as other trace minerals. Kelp is also known to boost the immune system and kill bacteria.

Yeast is a well known food supplement, in fact, many cat foods contain yeast as a primary ingredient. Yeast are fungi grown is a fermentation of carbohydrates and is high in vitamins and minerals, especially the B vitamins. Brewer's yeast is the most nutritious of the different kinds of yeast available.

Yogurt. Besides being a nourishing food on its own, yogurt contains beneficial bacteria that improve bowel functions. These bacteria help prevent intestinal infections, prevent diarrhea and kill problem causing bacteria. Yogurt is also known to boost the immune system and is thought to have anticancer properties.

IN CLOSING

Adding a supplement to your cat's food is a personal decision that should not be undertaken lightly. Too much supplementation can upset a previously balanced and complete diet. For example, raw eggs can hinder the absorption of biotin, a B-complex vitamin. Too much calcium and phosphorus can result in a myriad of health problems.

However, supplements added to the diet wisely can benefit your cat greatly, improving skin, coat, energy, stress resistance and overall health. The key to using supplements is to do so intelligently, researching the supplement and the food your cat eats. If you have any doubts, talk to the cat food manufacturer, and if the supplement you are adding is a commercially manufactured supplement, talk to that company's representative as well. If you see any detrimental changes in your cat's health, of course stop the supplement immediately and call your veterinarian.

NINE

HOMEMADE DIETS: SHOULD YOU COOK FOR YOUR CAT?

Cat owners who decide to cook for their cats do so for a variety of reasons. Sometimes a cat will have specific needs—such as food allergies—that cannot be satisfied by commercial foods. Sometimes the cat owner wishes the cat to eat according to the owner's nutritional or philosophical beliefs. Or the owner might be concerned about the ingredients that commercial cat foods contain.

The decision to feed a homemade diet is not one to be taken lightly. Today's cat foods are the result of much research—sometimes years of laboratory analysis and feeding trials. Replacing that research with an indiscriminate homemade diet can result in nutritional disaster. Even some nutritionists are hesitant about formulating their own diets. However, if you feel strongly about feeding your cat a home cooked diet, if care is taken and the cat's health is monitored closely, a homemade diet can work.

Change your cat over to a homemade diet slowly, over a period of three weeks, minimum. If you switch too quickly, your cat will suffer gastrointestinal upset, possibly including vomiting and diarrhea. The first week, feed three-quarters (75 percent) old food and one-quarter (25 percent) new food. The second week, feed 50/50. The third week, feed one-quarter old food and three-quarters new food. By the fourth week, you should be able to feed the new diet entirely.

One downfall of a homemade diet you should be aware of is that the diet is cooked and soft and therefore provides no chewing action, no gum stimulation and no dental benefits, except of course, those benefits provided internally by good nutrition. You will have to pay close attention to your cat's teeth, cleaning them on a regular basis.

INGREDIENTS TO AVOID

If you decide to formulate a homemade diet for your cat, there are some ingredients you should avoid.

Bones are one. Even though a hunting cat would eat some of the small bones of its prey, bones can be dangerous to cats. A bone could get stuck in the cat's mouth or throat, causing pain, injury or even choking. If swallowed, a bone can cause tremendous damage to the gastrointestinal tract. So avoid bones, even fish bones. Bone meal, however, is good for your cat, supplying many needed nutrients. Supplement the diet according to the directions on the package.

Although many cat owners seem to think their cat needs milk, many adult cats actually dislike it. Others cannot digest it well, suffering from diarrhea afterwards. If your cat likes milk and can tolerate it, a spoonful now and then is fine. A tablespoon of yogurt is even better.

Do not give your cat raw egg whites as they hamper the metabolism of many B vitamins, including biotin. Raw egg yolks are fine, though.

Don't feed your cat raw fish as it can be loaded with parasites, protozoa and bacteria. Raw fish also prevents the metabolism of some B vitamins, including B1.

Feed raw meat only sparingly, for the same reasons, as it, too, can hide potential health hazards. However, a helping of raw meat can sometimes tempt a non-eating cat into eating. See Chart 24.

Some cats like to sneak into the family dog's bowl. Although an occasional bite of dog food won't hurt, the nutritional needs of dogs and cats are different and a steady diet of dog food will threaten your cat's health.

MONITORING THE RESULTS

Just as with a commercial food, the test of the food is in the results it produces. If your cat has food allergies, you should start to see some change after about a week or two on the new diet. Your cat will not be "all better" but you should see some lessening of the symptoms. If the symptoms get worse or if new problems pop up, stop the new diet, go back to the old and call your veterinarian. You may need to adjust the contents; perhaps there is a food allergy you didn't know about.

Watch your cat's weight, too. Many cats are so thrilled with the new diet they act absolutely famished and will overeat if given the chance. If your cat gains weight after starting the new diet, decrease the amount of food slightly.

Keep in mind that diet is important but it is not the only thing that affects your cat's health. Keep track of your cat's health, what happens in the cat's environment and work with your veterinarian.

IN CLOSING

Charts 21 through 24 detail several different homemade diets. These were formulated by health-conscious cat owners or breeders who were concerned about the food their cats were eating. These people were not, however, veterinarians or dieticians, although several did consult with experts while formulating their diets.

Other homemade diets are available from other sources. In his book, *Pet Allergies: Remedies for an Epidemic* (Very Healthy Enterprises, 1986), Dr. Alfred Plechner has several different homemade diets, including hypoallergenic diets. Richard Pitcairn, DVM, PhD, and Susan Hubble Pitcairn, authors of *Dr. Pitcairn's Complete Guide to Natural Health for Dogs and Cats* (Rodale Press, 1982), list several homemade diets in their book.

Please consult with your veterinarian before starting your cat on a homemade diet, watch your cat carefully as you feed this diet, and keep your vet posted about any changes you notice in your cat's skin, coat, energy levels, teeth and overall health.

CHART 21
A BASIC HOMEMADE DIET

This is a basic diet for cats with no known food allergies.

Mix together in a big bowl:

1 pound ground meat (chicken, turkey, lamb) browned, drain off
   most of the fat

1 six-ounce can of tuna (canned in water, not oil)

1 medium potato, cooked, mashed

2 cups cooked whole grain brown rice

1/2 cup cooked oatmeal

1/2 cup cooked, mashed barley

1/2 cup grated carrots, raw

1/2 cup finely chopped raw green vegetables (broccoli, spinach,
   green beans)

2 tablespoon olive oil

2 tablespoons minced garlic

Serving size: About 3/4 cup for a 7-pound cat to about 1 1/2 cups for a
12-pound cat. Adjust the amounts depending upon your cat's appetite,
activity level, energy needs, weight gain or weight loss.

Add when serving:

Dash of sea kelp powder

Dash of bone meal

A vitamin/mineral supplement

Taurine supplement

Herbal supplements (depending upon your cat's needs)

Store in the refrigerator in the covered bowl, or divide into daily servings and store in the freezer, thawing a day or two at a time.

CHART 22
STRESS RECIPE

This recipe is good for cats under stress; cats going to shows, recuperating from illness, surgery or pregnant or lactating queens.

Mix together in a large bowl:

1 pound ground meat, browned, do not drain off fat (chicken, turkey)

1 six ounce can tuna (canned in water, not oil)

4 large eggs, hardboiled, shelled, crumbled

2 cups cooked whole grain brown rice

1 cup cooked oatmeal

1 large potato, cooked, finely chopped

1/4 cup wheat germ

1/2 cup raw grated carrot

1/2 cup chopped raw green vegetables

3 tablespoons olive oil

2 tablespoons minced garlic

Serving size: About 3/4 cup for a 7-pound cat to about 1 1/2 cups for a 12-pound cat. Adjust amounts according to your cat's needs, activity levels, health and weight.

Add when serving:

A teaspoon size spoonful of yogurt

Dash of yeast

A multivitamin/mineral tablet

250 mg vitamin C, ground into powder

Taurine supplement

Dash of sea kelp powder

Dash of bone meal

Herbal supplements (depending upon your cat's needs)

Store in the refrigerater in covered bowl or divide into daily servings and freeze.

CHART 23
A RECIPE FOR CATS WITH FOOD ALLERGIES

Before starting this diet, you should have an idea of what foods your cat is allergic to. The most common food items causing allergies for cats seem to be wheat and/or beef. However, every cat is different. You can have your veterinarian run allergy tests, or with your veterinarian's guidance, you can do some food elimination tests at home. Then depending upon what your cat is allergic to, you can make this diet suit your cat's needs. Obviously, if your cat is allergic to chicken, feed ground lamb instead. If your cat is allergic to eggs, drop them from the recipe and use another protein source, such as a milk product.

Mix together in a big bowl:

1 pound ground meat (chicken, turkey or lamb) browned, drain off all but a little of the fat

1 eight ounce can cooked, deboned salmon

2 eggs, hard-boiled, shelled, crumbled

3 cups cooked whole grain brown rice

1 cup cooked oatmeal

1/2 cup finely grated carrot, raw

1/2 cup finely chopped green vegetables, raw (broccoli, spinach, green beans)

2 tablespoons olive oil

1 tablespoon minced garlic

Serving size: Feed about 3/4 cup to a 7-pound cat, up to 1 1/2 cups for a 12-pound cat. Amounts will vary depending upon your cat's needs, energy levels, health and weight.

CHART 23, Continued

Add when serving:

A multivitamin/mineral tablet

Dash of sea kelp powder

Dash of bone meal

Taurine supplement

Herbal supplements (based upon your cat's needs)

Store in refrigerator, or store the food in plastic bags, divided into daily portions and store in the freezer.

CHART 24
YOU SAY YOUR CAT WON'T EAT?

Sometimes cats won't eat when they most need to, such as when recuperating from surgery or illness. This recipe is designed to tempt any cat; feed it when you need your cat to eat or when it needs a little extra boost. This is NOT a food to feed on a daily basis.

Mix together in a bowl:

1 cup lean, raw ground beef

1 raw egg yolk (no white)

1 tablespoon tofu

1 tablespoon finely grated carrot

1 tablespoon canned corn

1 tablespoon cooked oatmeal or 1 tablespoon cooked pasta

Dash of garlic salt

Serving size: Depends upon how much the cat needs, how much you can get it to eat and the cat's size, health and so on.

Add when serving:

Dash of bone meal

Dash of sea kelp powder

Additional note: If your cat likes catnip, a dash of catnip mixed into the food will sometimes tempt the cat into eating.

TEN

CAT FOOD TREATS

Just as with treats for people, some cat treats are pure junk food, full of corn syrup, meat scraps and cereal fillers. Some treats use some pretty strong preservatives; something many cat owners are concerned about. Other treats are actually good nutrition. But all of these nibbles, cookies, snacks and other good stuff—anything your cat eats—must be taken into account when considering the cat's overall nutrition.

SEMIMOIST TREATS. These treats are very palatable; cats love them. However, semimoist treats, like semimoist cat foods, have a higher sugar content than other treats. They are usually higher in additives, too, especially artificial colors and flavors. If you are concerned with your cat's diet, make sure to read the labels on these treats.

One of the most popular semimoist treats is Pounce, made by the Quaker Oats Company. The primary ingredients of Pounce Beef Treats are wheat, eggs and liver. Crude protein is listed as 20 percent, fat is 7 percent, fiber is 1.5 percent and moisture is 35 percent. Pounce does not list sugar as a primary ingredient but does list several preservatives, including potassium sorbate and BHA. This Pounce also includes FD&C Red No. 40.

Another semimoist treat is called Catty Shack. The Catty Shack Shrimp & Tuna flavor lists as its primary ingredients: liver, chicken by-products, poultry by-products, corn and fishmeal. Corn syrup is the eighth ingredient. This treat also uses BHA preservatives and has Red No. 40 and Yellow Nos. 5 and 6.

KIBBLE-TYPE TREATS. Hard cat food, kibble-type treats are very popular, both with cats and their owners. These treats come in every size, shape, color and flavor imaginable. Some treats are round, others are square. There are big treats, little treats, beef flavored, liver flavored; the list is unending.

Many of these treats are actually good nutrition, not as a complete food, but as a supplement to your cat's diet. For example, Jackie's Deli Style Cat Snacks, Liver Flavor, have as the first few ingredients: wheat, liver, water, soy, glycerine, dried whey, chicken liver and yeast. The guaranteed analysis is 19 percent protein, 8 percent fat, 1.7 percent fiber, 34 percent moisture and 4 percent ash.

Pounce Tartar Control Treats are harder, kibble-type treats made to help scrape tartar off the cat's teeth as the treats are being eaten. Primary ingredients include corn, poultry by-products meal wheat and animal digest. These treats do include the preservatives BHA as well as tocopherols.

SPECIAL TREATS. Because treats are such big business and because cat owners want to give their cats something special, many companies have responded with special treats. Several companies sell small plastic bowls of potting soil preplanted with wheat or other grass seeds. Once the cat's owner wets the potting soil and the seeds sprout, the cat can nibble on the fresh green grass.

Catnip toys and treats are very popular. Although catnip doesn't effect or attract all cats, the cats who are attracted to it love it. Dignified old cats will roll around on the floor like a kitten! Toys are available stuffed with catnip, or you can buy the dried herb plain. Plant nurseries that sell herbs will usually carry catnip, too, and this herb is easy to grow in the garden or on a windowsill.

Freeze dried liver treats, normally sold as dog treats, are eagerly eaten by many cats. Miracle Pet Freeze Dried Liver Treats by Specialty Pet Products describes its treats as freeze-dried, all natural liver treats, 100 percent pure with no additives, preservatives, artificial colors or flavors. Many other companies make freeze-dried liver treats; just read the label so that you know what is in the treat.

TREATS FROM THE KITCHEN. One of my first cats loved canned corn. If I wanted him to do something he didn't want to do, all I had to do was open a can of corn. I have since found many cats like corn and have found that there are many potential cat treats in the kitchen. Some cats love to nibble on the green husk from an ear of corn, others like alfalfa sprouts. Scrambled eggs, cooked squash, elbow macaroni or even cooked oatmeal can all be a treat if your cat likes them.

Again, as with any treat, add treats carefully, making sure not to upset the balance of the cat's overall diet. However, if your cat seems to crave some greens or vegetables, let him have some. As we discussed earlier, hunting cats that devour their prey will also eat the entrails of their prey, which may contain a variety of plant matter. Cats that do not hunt may be missing out on this natural part of their diet.

WHAT *NOT* TO FEED YOUR CAT

Most nutritionists agree that you should avoid or severely limit your cat's sugar intake. Sugar is empty calories to your cat, just as it is for people, and treats loaded with sugar are very poor nutrition.

Avoid chocolate, too. Chocolate contains caffeine and theobromine, which people can digest; dogs and cats cannot. Different kinds of chocolate have different chemical contents. One ounce of dark, bitter baker's chocolate could poison a 10-pound cat. Sweet milk chocolate, the kind we usually have in candy bars, is not quite as lethal but it's still dangerous.

Most veterinarians also recommend that cat owners do not give their cats bones. Although it seems that stripping the meat off bones should be natural for cats, most veterinarians have performed innumerable surgeries to repair the intestinal tracts of cats who have ingested sharp bone pieces.

IN CLOSING

The decision to give your cat treats is a personal one. Some people do not want to give their cat "people" food because they don't want the cat to beg when at the dinner table. Other people enjoy giving treats. It's strictly up to you but if you do decide to give treats, monitor the number of treats given so you don't upset the balance of your cat's diet. Watch your cat's weight, too.

If you are one of those cat owners who is very concerned about artificial colorings, flavorings and preservatives, make sure you read the labels on the treats. As was mentioned in this chapter, most of the commercial treats contain artificial colorings, flavorings and preservatives.

Finding the treat your cat considers special may take some searching, too. Each and every cat has different tastes, as do people. What one cat considers to be a special treat may be scorned by another cat. It may take some experimentation to find that extra special treat.

CHART 25
COMMERCIAL CAT FOOD TREATS:
NUTRITIONAL COMPARISONS

Product	First Five Ingredients
Bonkers Cat Treats	
Protein 25%	1. liver
Fat 10%	2. chicken by-products
Fiber 2%	3. poultry by-products
Moisture 30%	4. corn
Ash *(not listed)*	5. gelantized corn
Catty Shack Gourmet	
Protein 25%	1. liver
Fat 10%	2. chicken by-products
Fiber 2%	3. poultry by-products
Moisture 30%	4. corn
Ash *(not listed)*	5. gelatanized corn
Jackie's Cat Snacks Chicken & Cheese	
Protein 19%	1. wheat flour
Fat 8%	2. chicken
Fiber 1.7%	3. water
Moisture 34%	4. soy flour
Ash 4%	5. glycerine
Jackie's Cat Snacks Liver	
Protein 19%	1. wheat flour
Fat 8%	2. liver
Fiber 1.7%	3. water
Moisture 34%	4. soy flour
Ash 4%	5. glycerine

CHART 25, CONTINUED

Product	First Five Ingredients

Pounce Semimoist Beef

Protein 20%	1. wheat flour
Fat 7%	2. eggs
Fiber 1.5%	3. liver
Moisture 35%	4. beef
Ash *(not listed)*	5. wheat gluten

Pounce Tartar Control Tuna

Protein 29%	1. ground corn
Fat 8%	2. poultry by-products
Fiber 3%	3. corn gluten meal
Moisture 10%	4. ground wheat
Ash *(not listed)*	5. yeast

Whisker Lickin's Fishy's

Protein 24%	1. liver
Fat 8.5%	2. wheat flour
Fiber 1%	3. poultry by-products
Moisture 36%	4. corn gluten meal
Ash *(not listed)*	5. water

Whisker Lickin's Tartar Control

Protein 31%	1. poultry by-products
Fat 10%	2. corn
Fiber 4%	3. wheat flour
Moisture 11%	4. corn gluten meal
Ash *(not listed)*	5. animal digest

BIBLIOGRAPHY, ADDITIONAL READING AND RESEARCH

Ackerman, DVM, PhD, Lowell. "Dietary Supplements: Therapy for the Skin," *Dog World* (September 1994): 18-20.

American Association of Feed Control Officials. Georgia Department of Agriculture, 404-656-3637.

Ammer, Christine. *It's Raining Cats and Dogs . . .* New York: Bantam Books, 1989.

Anderson, Moira. "Food for Thought," *Dog Fancy* 18, no. 5 (April 1987).

Becker, Ross. "What's Really in Dog Food?" *The Dog Food Book,* 2nd edition. Austin, TX: *Good Dog!,* 1995.

Braly, MD, James. *Dr. Braly's Food Allergy and Nutrition Revolution.* New York: Keats Publishing, Inc., 1992.

Cargill, MA, MBA, MS, John. "Feed That Dog!" *Dog World* nos. 7-10 (July 1993, August 1993, September 1993): 24-29, 10-16, 14-22.

Carper, Jean. *The Food Pharmacy.* New York: Bantam Books, 1988.

Comfort, David. *The First Pet History of the World.* New York: A Fireside Book, Simon & Schuster, 1994.

Curtis, Patricia. *The Indoor Cat.* New York: A Pedigree Book, 1981.

Dick Van Patten's Natural Balance Pet Foods, PO Box 7956-425, Canoga Park, CA 91309.

Dolan, Edward. *Animal Folklore.* New York: Ivy Books, 1992.

Donoghue, DVM, Susan. "Nutrition: Gastrointestinal Disorders," *AKC Gazette* 110, no. 11 (November 1993).

———. "Nutrition: Cancer Prevention and Treatment," *AKC Gazette* 111, no. 4 (April 1994).

———. "Nutrition: Vitamin and Mineral Supplements," *AKC Gazette* 110, no. 10 (October 1993).

———. "Nutrition: Feeding Different Breeds," *AKC Gazette* 110, no. 6 (June 1993).

———. "Nutrition: Stressed Out Dogs," *AKC Gazette* 109, no. 8 (August 1992).

Ducommun, Debbie. "Dog Food Debate," *Dog Fancy* 25, no.11 (November 1994) 41-45.

Dunn, Jr., DVM, T. J. "Food for Thought," *Dog World* 80, no. 4 (April 1995) 50-52.

Dunne, Lavon J. *Nutrition Almanac; Third Edition.* New York: McGraw-Hill Publishing Co. 1990.

Frazier, Anitra. *The New Natural Cat.* New York: A Plume Book, 1990.

Gearhart, DVM, Martha. "Veterinary Viewpoint: Deciphering Pet Food Labels," *The Pet Dealer* 42, no. 7 (July 1993) 20-24, 84.

Geslewitz, Gina "RX for Mealtime," *The Pet Dealer* 42, no. 12 (December 1993) 54-60.

Ginsberg, Susan. "Pets Battle the Bulge," *Animals* (Nov/December 1991) 5-8.

Glinsky, Ph.D., Martin. "Pet Food Fallacies." *The Dog Food Book*, 2nd edition. Austin, TX: *Good Dog!* May/June 1995.

Guidry, Virginia Parker. "Looking at Labels," *Dog Fancy* 26, no. 5 (May 1995) 46-53.

Haas, MD, Elson M. *Staying Healthy with Nutrition.* Berkeley, CA Celestial Arts Publishing Co. 1992.

"Harper's Illustrated Handbook of Cats," Harper Perennial, 1993.

Hart, Benjamin, DVM, PhD. "Feline Behavior." Davis, CA.: Veterinary Practice Pulishing, 1980.

Hill's Pet Products, PO Box 148, Topeka, KS 66601 (913) 354-8523.

Humphries, Jim, DVM. *Dr. Jim's Animal Clinic for Cats.* New York: Howell Book House, 1994.

The Iams Company, 7250 Poe Avenue, Dayton, OH (800) 525-4267.

Kallfelz, Francis DVM. "Nutrition and Your Kitten," *Cats USA* 1996 Annual.

Kritsick, DVM, Steve. "Nutrition and Health: You Get What You Pay For," *AKC Gazette* 102, no. 11 (November 1985) 22-23.

Lang, Laura. "Evaluating Dog Foods," *AKC Gazette* 105, no. 10 (October 1988) 48-52.

Lewis, DVM, PhD, Lon D. "Feeding: Methods, Types and Problems," *Bloodlines* (Mar/April 1993).

Long, Patricia. "The Vitamin Wars," *Health* (May/June 1993) 45-54.

Ludeman, PhD, Kate and Louise Henderson. *Do-It-Yourself Allergy Analysis Handbook.* New Canaan, CT: Keats Publishing, Inc., 1979.

Nutro Products, Inc. 445 Wilson Way, City of Industry, CA 91744 818-968-0532.

Pet Food Institute and Nutrition Assurance Program, (800) 851-0769.

Phelps, Karen. "Canine Nutrition: Fads, Facts and Fallacies." *Dog World* 70, no. 1 (January 1985) 11, 87-93.

Pitcairn, DVM, PhD, Richard H. and Susan Hubble Pitcairn. *Natural Health for Dogs and Cats* Emmaus, PA: Rodale Press, 1982.

Plechner, DVM, Alfred J. and Martin Zucker. *Pet Allergies: Remedies for an Epidemic.* Inglewood, CA: Very Healthy Enterprises, 1986.

Ryan, Dr. Thomas. "Zinc: A Precious Mineral," *Dog Fancy* 16, no. 8 (August 1985) 46-47.

Shaffer, PhD, Martin. *Life After Stress.* Chicago: Contemporary Books, Inc., 1983.

Shojai, Amy. "From Concept to Can." *AKC Gazette* 111, no. 10 (October 1994) 48-52.

————. "Beating Cancer," *Dog World* 80, no.1 (January 1995) 24-26

————. "Reading the Dog Food Label," *Dog World* 77, no. 9 (September 1992) 14-18.

Sokolowski, DVM, PhD, James H. and Anthony M. Fletcher, DVM. *Basic Guide to Canine Nutrition; Fifth Edition.* Chicago: Gaines Professional Services, 1987.

Source Micronutrients Source, Inc. 101 Fowler Road, N. Branford, CT 06471 (203) 488-6400.

Smith, DVM, Carin. "RX Therapeutic Diet," *AKC Gazette* 108, no. 10 (October 1991) 78-82.

Thurston, Mary. "Feeding Fido in the Good Old Days," *Dog World* 77, no. 6 (June 1992) 14-20.

————. "Dog Food Around the World," *Good Dog!* 6, no. 1 (Jan/Feb 1993).

Vital Energy #1 All Systems, PO Box 1330, Ojai, CA 93023 (800) 525-7998.

Warzecha, Mary. "Canine Cuisine," *Dog Fancy* 22, no. 7 (July 1991) 67-70.

————. "The $100 Dinner." *Dog Fancy* 19, no. 4 (April 1988) 17-20.

Weitzman, Nan. "How to Buy Dog Food," *The Dog Food Book*, 2nd edition. Austin, TX *Good Dog!* 1995.

Wilford, DVM, Christine. "Allergies," *Dog Fancy* 25, no. 5 (May 1994) 47-51.

Willard, PhD, Thomas. "What are We Really Feeding Our Dogs?" *AKC Gazette* 109, no. 7 (July 1992) 46-49.

INDEX